Fact and Folklore

Social and Psychological Foundations of Teaching

Gerald Kushel
Constant A. Madon

Graduate School of Education
C. W. Post Center
Long Island University

John Wiley & Sons, Inc., New York · London · Sidney · Toronto

to Selma, Joan and Lynne
and
to Sylvia

Library of Congress Cataloging in Publication Data:

Kushel, Gerald.
  Fact and folklore.

  Includes bibliographies.
  1. Teaching as a profession. 2. Educational sociology. 3. Education—United States. I. Madon, Constant A., joint author. II. Title.

LB1775.K79 1974   371.1'02   74-1211
ISBN 0-471-51108-0
ISBN 0-471-51106-4 (pbk.)

Printed in the United States of America

10-9 8 7 6 5 4 3 2 1

PREFACE

Emotional, often-contradictory statements have been made about our educational system: "We need more innovations in our school!" "My children need a more stable school system!" "Kids learn best in an informal, open environment." "They need more, not less structure!" "On with the *new* math!" "Return to the three Rs!" And so on.

This textbook, especially the case method that it utilizes, is designed to help the serious student of education to find his way through the maze of folklore and unfounded opinion concerning teaching toward a semblance of truth.

Optimal development in education is not based on seeking answers to empty questions but on responsibly raising the *right* questions. Therefore, our premise here is that new teaching directions should be based on careful examination of relevant theory and a critical review of current practices. Current practices, gleaned from the commentary and reflections of experienced teachers and administrators, are the starting point. Many practitioners were interviewed, and the substance of these "real life" interviews was developed into 15 carefully chosen thematic selections or cases. These cases, built on practical experience, contain considerable folk wisdom, and the limited facts provide a resource for critical examination.

Although the case-study approach is a valid avenue toward "the truth," it does not necessarily produce ready answers to the problems that continue to plague teachers. However, it will stimulate the student to ask questions, and we hope that these questions will be pointed and sophisticated.

Gerald Kushel
Constant A. Madon

THIS BOOK AND A WAY TO USE IT

This book is divided into four sections: I. Background and Foundations of Teaching, II. Today's Student, III. The Process, and IV. The Teacher. Each of these sections leads off with a comprehensive, theoretical review followed by lively issue-laden cases and relevant questions. Therefore, we recommend the following approach to using this text:

1. Briefly review the theoretical material in each section.
2. Study carefully a case or two in the same section.
3. Return to the theoretical material but this time purposefully and with questions in mind.
4. If further information or research is needed, refer to the procedures enumerated in Appendix A, Guide to "Answer Finding" in Education.

G.K.
C.A.M.

ACKNOWLEDGMENTS

We express our gratitude to the many teachers who shared the confidences with us that form much of the substance of this work. In addition, we thank colleagues who generously offered comments and encouragement, the C. W. Post Research Committee for a helpful research grant, and the Graduate School of Education for the special assistance of Jane Cohen, Judy Wilcox, Betty Nanos, Virginia Kursch, and Mimi Fetta.

G.K.
C.A.M.

CONTENTS

Section I BACKGROUND AND FOUNDATIONS OF TEACHING

What is meant by the foundations of teaching and education? At the outset we discover that fixed parameters of the body of knowledge often referred to as "foundations of education" are not at all easily established but instead tend to emanate from many forces at work in society. The problem, therefore, is in sifting out the particular societal factors that bear quite specifically on the learning-teaching process [1] and in utilizing this perspective to modify and hopefully improve education. In this introduction, a process of inquiry is initiated where the organized disciplines are used as points of reference, some important concepts related to education are identified, and the expression of these ideas in the school setting are then discussed.

In the two teacher-centered selections taken from real life that follow this introduction, you will have the opportunity to see and examine the interplay of the various physical and social science disciplines in a holistic context. In fact, all 15 thematic selections portrayed in this book offer lucid testimony to the interplay of the various disciplines as they relate to education.

Comprehending, for example, the connection between the

[1] *The student is inevitably engaged in some processes of learning, even before being exposed to teaching, therefore, we have had learning precede teaching.*

1

social science disciplines of political science or economics to Case 2, "Lace Tablecloths and Silver Tea Service for All," would not necessarily be clear to the casual observer. But the sensitive and serious student in education should be able to readily discern that (1) the politics of power most certainly impinge on the day-to-day work of Helen D. and quite specifically to her bold, controversial act of breaking the picket line, and (2) the school in the poor side of town is a victim of the economic principle connected with the distribution of goods— no lace tablecloths.

In fact, both of these small instances can be understood not only through application of some of the light shed from political science and economics, but also from sociology, history, and philosophy. Each instance is replete with questions of such areas as values, power, "ins and outs," and distribution of goods. Sometimes the connection is subtle . . . at other times, all too obvious. In this introduction, then, the physical sciences as well as the social science disciplines of philosophy, psychology, anthropology, sociology, political science, economics, and history are each examined to identify the societal forces that materially affect education. These forces are termed "leading indicators" that, when taken together, form a tentative whole.

It is important to note that progress in all the physical and social sciences is not uniform; thus we find gaps, overlaps, rapid progressions and slower ones, outstanding strengths, and notable weaknesses. Developments in these disciplines tend to lie outside the sphere of the school, and it is the teacher's function to devise ways of adapting and integrating these new ideas into her daily teaching. The sciences are an example of extremely rapid developments produced by our technology at a faster pace than the average person can assimilate them. The trappings of technological progress (i.e., computers, teaching machines, and audiovisual materials of assorted varieties) are found in many classrooms, but the teacher has yet to devise a comprehensive plan for students to benefit fully from them. Nevertheless, the successful teacher needs to establish a new methodology for incorporating these "tools of learning" into the larger framework of the learning-teaching process.

EFFECTS OF PROGRESS IN THE SCIENCES

Progress in the sciences has influenced and, in fact, helped shape other forces in our society, such as the rapid growth of urbanization and changes in demographic patterns. Urbanization has brought with it attendant problems for the teacher. A concentration of poor and disadvantaged youth is found mainly in our inner cities. The teacher is faced with having to find ways of adapting the basic tools of reading and arithmetic for a student, who, at the outset, needs special help with his own unique problem of establishing an identity and then realizing his own potential.

Demographic patterns have shown a larger and larger concentration of our population in the megalopolis or urban suburban centers, reaching up and down the east and west coasts and inward across the Great Lakes. As a result, our school systems have grown in size in direct proportion to these population shifts. Teachers find themselves enmeshed in a large, bureaucratic organization and must strive to reach their students on a human level when such forces as scheduling and red tape mediate against this. They also find that the division of labor found in the urban society has permeated the school, and they must adjust to many specialists and administrators, each with a specialized function.

THE SOCIAL SCIENCES

The social sciences are windows through which we examine society. Each window has a special tint that filters certain aspects while leaving others to be interpreted differently. The human condition is both individual and social; it is deeply personal and uniquely universal. For the teacher, the implications of these ideas are highly significant. She is, in every sense, committed to the concept of freedom within our democratic framework. Her authority rests on her knowledge as an expert in her profession and from the mandate of the community. She values individual differences among her students and strives to enhance those special qualities that each person possesses. Nevertheless, while these are ideals for the teacher to strive toward, she is, in fact, faced with the ramifications of a "value crisis" occurring within the larger society. The cry is "relevance," and programs or curricula that were once valued as being worthwhile and necessary for an education are being questioned and, in some cases, discarded. The role of the teacher as a "giver of knowledge" or expert has undergone a metamorphosis. She can no longer hide behind her expertise. Knowledge is to be absorbed by the learner rather than given by an authority figure. The emphasis has shifted from the teacher as the central figure to the learner. While remaining the single most valuable resource in the school, the teacher's role is now one of helping youngsters acquire knowledge on their own. Hence, the authority of the teacher once derived from that of the expert has diminished considerably.

PHILOSOPHY AND EDUCATION

All contemporary theories and positions have their roots in philosophy. What is education? Why educate? Who should be educated? How should we educate? These and questions such as these permeate this text. Answers, or positions, are derived from philosophical premises. For example, the question: How should we educate? requires a philosophical view of the inherent nature of man. A permissive education presumes goodness. Is man essentially "good" or "evil"? Define "good." These are largely axiological, value-laden issues.

Educational philosophy is viewed as the application of traditional philosophical thought to educational issues. The three major concerns of all philosophy are: What is reality? What is truth? What is value?

What people casually profess and do often portrays their educational philosophy. Which one of the following quotes, in your view, describes the best kind of education for American children?

1. "School should be child centered, largely noncompetitive, life itself, rather than preparation for life."

2. "Education should be about the same for everyone. There are, after all, certain classical truths that every educated person should master."

3. "Learning is hard work, and the teachers should see to it that the child develops a proper mental discipline."

4. "Society is in drastic need of repair, and good education implies social action, not merely ideas for the sake of ideas."

Certainly these positions require a deep personal and thoughtful search. Each, on the surface, has merit. Some however, are juxtaposed. They represent well-conceived and widely discussed theoretical positions rooted in educational philosophy. The first position—the child-centered school—illustrates progressivism, drawing on the pragmatic philosophers. The second—perennialism—emanates from classical realists and their models of truth. The third implies a position known as essentialism. Essentialism, as a philosophical view, maintains that there are certain essentials all men must know. The fourth quote illustrates Brameld's doctrine of reconstructionism (i.e., the primary purpose of education is to move rapidly toward the reconstruction of society).

Each of the 15 selections in this book raise serious philosophical issues. When Martin Graham (Selection 7), in speaking of youngsters, says, "Oh, they'll take advantage all right and I can't blame them for that," what is he suggesting about the nature of man? What philosophical tenets are implicit in his view? The central issue in Selection 1, a selection appended to this particular introduction, focuses on "the purposes of education" . . . an issue clearly imbedded within the realm of philosophy. In Selection 12, do the ends (greater departmental efficiency) justify the means (old Blake's dismissal)?

As Kneller (1971) points out, "philosophy attempts to establish a coherence throughout the whole domain of experience" (p. 201). Phenix (1962) contends, "Every person who has a reflectively held point of view about basic values and assumptions in education, has a philosophy of education" (p. 4). The key here is, "reflectively held."

The aim of this text, the selections, the teacher-centered cases, and the questions raised, aim to induce reflection. The philosophers, ancient and modern—Plato, Socrates, Comenius, Locke, Rousseau, Kant, Mill, Dewey, Buber, and Russell, to name a few—can render a needed perspective on the transient issues of the day. The student of education, drawing on the vision of great individual philosophers and the useful modes of thought ranging from classical realism to experimentalism and existentialism can begin to comprehend the often enormous issues found between-the-lines in these teacher-centered selections.

PSYCHOLOGY AND EDUCATION

The discipline of psychology is concerned with the mind and behavior of the individual. While developmental and educational psychology will be discussed in detail in Sections II and III, it is important to note here that research in psychology has had a notable impact on the activities of the teacher. For example, we have developed the techniques of drill and practice from Thorndike's stimulus-response theory. More recently, the theories of Bruner have given us insights into the structure of knowledge and the notion of conceptual learning. And Skinner's operant conditioning schema has introduced us to programmed instruction and behavior modification.

ANTHROPOLOGY AND EDUCATION

The anthropologist examines the whole range of human behavior. For such a total way of life, he uses the term "culture"—the whole system of interrelated behavior produced by a people (Honigmann, 1959). One facet of the study of the American culture has been a focus on ethnic minorities and their relationships to the larger society. We tend to adhere to the concept of "cultural pluralism"—that each ethnic group has its own unique qualities and that they should be recognized and should flourish within the whole of American life. The effect of these ideas has had a significant impact upon the school and its curriculum. In some instances, new courses focusing on black, Mexican, Puerto Rican, Chinese, Japanese, and Indian Americans have been developed or the contributions of these ethnic minorities incorporated into existing curricula. Notwithstanding these accomplishments, however, a large proportion of schools are still faced with the persistent problem of presenting a more balanced view of the contributions and issues related to American minorities. The individual teacher, particularly in the social sciences, is faced with an important value question regarding first whether or not to include material on minority Americans in her class discussions and then to determine the extent of coverage in relation to the total curriculum. There is the whole question of whether or not time should be spent on the contributions of minority Americans if the school population is essentially white and middle class. If suburban youngsters are removed from the problems of ghettos, should the teacher attempt to expose the harsh realities of ghetto life to her students? Should she emphasize the contributions of minority Americans who have been successful in our society and downplay such issues as poverty, crime, housing, and drugs that are a part of everyday life of the ghetto youngster? Or vice versa, are the issues more important than the contributions of those Americans who have "made it" in our society. While one recognizes that a synthesis rather than either-or positions are desirable, there still remains a large proportion of teachers and administrators who have not yet come to grips with these basic questions.

SOCIOLOGY AND EDUCATION

Sociologists attempt to analyze and describe human groups (Rose, 1965). On the national scene, youth groups have attracted notable attention. We have seen a focus on problem areas connected with our youth such as alienation, drugs, sex, school dropouts, the disadvantaged, and military service.

While these factors will be discussed in Section II—"Today's Student"—it is important to note that scholars and researchers have provided insights into today's youth and their problems. For the teacher and administrator there is the larger concern of providing a set of experiences that will alleviate many of the symptoms of these problems. Suffice to say that in the past we have been overly concerned with academic achievement, perhaps, at the expense of basic human development. We have been caught up with the need to prepare youngsters for college at the expense of preparing them for life. And we have tried to impose adult values on our youth. To be successful with today's youth, educators must invent new ways of assimilating them into society. More emphasis will have to be given to personal-human relationships and the development of self-concept and self-awareness. And there should be more time devoted to preparing our youth to live in today's complex society. Therefore, our traditional curricula will have to change to accommodate the differing needs of today's young people.

POLITICAL SCIENCE AND EDUCATION

The scope of political science is the study of power—in other words, with the phenomena of command that appears in society (Sorauf, 1965). Power is observed from several viewpoints such as the activities over which legal government exercises control, how the power to make decisions is distributed, and the distribution of power in formal and informal institutions. Our society has experienced a subtle and gradual shift in the distribution of power to make decisions away from central government toward specific pressure groups. A second phenomena is that these informal groups with special interests have become politicized and have influenced our national decision making. Witness, for example, the pressure groups in such areas as energy, space exploration, and housing and their impact on federal legislation. Similarly, the traditional decision-making powers of state departments of education and local school boards have given way to a host of special interest groups. Such were the pressures brought about by the war in

Vietnam, the Black Power movement, the ecology issues, youth protests, and whatever local issues tended to surface in a given community. Hence, the school not only was concerned with the curriculum as mandated by the state or the local board of education but also with the myriad of attendant problems generated by the community and, indeed, the world. It is safe to say that, by and large, schools were unprepared for this new kind of challenge. As a result, boards of education and administrators were forced to react rather than act. They were clearly on the defensive. The resulting confusion has tended to permeate every facet of the learning-teaching process. Once again, questions were raised. Should the school follow a conservative course and continue with the established curriculum, or should the issues of the community influence, mediate, and even change the course of education in a given community? Should the teacher ignore the issues or should she use her classroom as a forum for their discussion? Should the student act as catalyst in the change process or simply follow the established curriculum? Should the school ignore, mediate, or submit to the pressure groups within the community? It is not clear how these problems will be resolved. It is apparent, however, that the "old politics" of the school and the community are dead. For the most part, the textbook concepts of school-community relations of the 1950s and 1960s are past history. What we need is a redefinition and reconstruction of the relationships existing between a school and the community it serves.

ECONOMICS AND EDUCATION

The center of economic study is the choice-making process, and three kinds of activity are studied: the production, the exchange, and the consumption of goods, each characterized by particular institutions and activities (Martin and Miller, 1965). Due in part to a serious energy shortage, Americans are adopting a new set of values relative to the exchange and consumption of goods. We have, for example, a trend toward the purchase of smaller, more functional automobiles. Since automobiles, next to housing, account for a large proportion of the consumer's dollar, the trend is, indeed, significant. Similarly, the overall movement toward economy and efficiency has had its impact on the schools. Several innovations are taking place aimed at making education either more economical or more efficient or both. Included are differentiated staffing, behavioral objectives, and education vouchers.

Through differentiated staffing, a hierarchy of trained personnel is established from master teacher through five or six levels to teacher aide. By hiring semiprofessional personnel at a lower salary to perform certain tasks within the school structure, it is possible to reduce the adult-pupil ratio and thus increase the amount of time given to each student.

To increase the efficiency of learning, we attempt to measure outputs in terms of demonstrated behavior under the assumption that learning packages have been developed that lead the student toward a specific behavior. He may, for example, be required to demonstrate his knowledge through written exercises or through performances of various types.

Through the education voucher, parents are allotted a sum of money equal to the amount spent on their child's education, and they can decide where to enroll their child. In so doing, the parents are able to choose which school, in their opinion, offers the best education for the money allotted.

In these experiments, the economics concepts of producer-consumer have been employed in an attempt to find alternatives to our traditional educational patterns. Research in these areas is still going on, and any conclusions, at this point, do not present clear trends regarding the desirability of using "economic tools" in the learning-teaching process.

HISTORY AND EDUCATION

History is a study of past human events (Commager, 1965). As such, it provides patterns of what has occurred and, in many regards, sets the stage for the present and the future. Education in the United States has evolved as a free and public function. Furthermore, it has evolved as a state rather than federal function. These three concepts do, indeed, set the stage for present and future directions in education. It is expected, for example, that free public education will be supported through taxation. Educators and parents look to the state for guidelines in fiscal and curricular matters.

While history does sketch a rough outline for those of us living in the present, it cannot predict the dimensions of the various forces at work nor their impact on the future. Only an enlightened community can chart the course of the future. It is, therefore, incumbent on the leaders in education to present the trends and forces at work in society to the community as a whole, so that decisions about the future of education can be made in concert and insure for each child an education that will serve him in the coming decades.

In summary, this introduction has attempted to establish the idea that relatively few of the "foundations of teaching" lie strictly within the control of the school but instead are reflections of the orchestration of forces existing in the larger society. Much of the raw material for developing curricula and methodology is to be found in the pure and social sciences. Usually, conceptual advances in the various disciplines precede actual practice, and it is the educator's task to bridge the gap between knowledge and practice. Since the development of new knowledge is an ongoing process, so, too, must the school evolve ways of adapting and incorporating it into the learning-teaching process. An additional factor is the complexity of the learning-teaching process itself. The introduction to Section III will deal with the process in more detail. The main focus here was to present a framework and a set of guidelines for searching out significant trends that can have an impact on the future of education.

The vignettes that follow are intended to amplify points of conflict, many of which arise from the gap between knowledge gleaned from the various disciplines and actual classroom practice. We hope that they will stimulate further inquiry into the problem of educating our youth for the future.

Theme 1 **Directions of American Education**

Few persons, indeed, would dispute that predicting the future of American education is difficult, yet imperative. In predicting wisely, it is essential that we carefully examine both past and present conditions. What significant ideas, persons, and movements have contributed to the present condition of American education? Which of these hold most promise for the future? What lies ahead for the balance of the 1970s? The 1980s? The year 2001?

Brian Josephs, a middle-aged principal, shares some of his personal observations and anxieties as he contemplates "School in the Days Ahead."

Selection 1   SCHOOL DAYS: 2001

> *Principal:*   Brian Josephs
> *Age:*   43
> *Experience:*   21 years as teacher and administrator, elementary and secondary

I'm not clear as to what's ahead for American education, but I think we may have hit our stride somewhere around the 1940s and perhaps the early 1950s. We were probably doing a pretty good job, at least for those times. But then, I think in about the late 1950s, many of us began to realize that we were not really doing everything that we should have been doing.

You see, then we were concerned with student apathy and we, as professional educators, suddenly became terribly worried because the kids seemed, and were, completely disinterested in our schools and what the schools seemed to stand for. We, ourselves, weren't very sure why apathy was so pervasive. As I recall, many of us blamed it on poor John Dewey and got into the worn-out debate about progressive versus traditional and all that. The causes, however, were difficult to identify. My own view is, that the general quality of teaching and school administration just wasn't good enough to make school interesting. The quality of the product was quite far from tops. And then, in the 1960s, it suddenly occurred to us that the world was rapidly changing. The moderately content and placid 1950s moved to the violent 1960s. It was then that some of us in the schools discovered that we could no longer continue to separate political and social developments in America from the schools in America.

I believe that in the 1940s and 1950s, the schools were a sanctuary

13

. . . a nice comfortable shelter, away from many of the cruel realities of life in the world. And, in the 1960s, we thought we could continue, but events like the assassination of Kennedy and King, the
Vietnam war, the Kent State tragedy, and the black revolution all
highlighted the fact that we in education were most certainly not
doing at all that we should or could be doing. In fact, it was the
kids who tried to bring the facts of life to those of us who call ourselves professional educators. And yet, some of us in education still
aren't getting the message.

The kids really tried to bring reality to us. They said, "Listen you
guys, it's a whole new world out there. You've got to change. You've
got to think differently; you've got to look at us differently, and furthermore, it may already be too late, because the world's not going
to wait any longer."

And change became necessary, simply because the schools, these
past 10, 20 years have not been responding to the times. Oh, we've
made the most marvelous, beautiful statements that one could wish
for about democracy, preparing students for life and all that, but
we didn't really do the kind of job that was needed. The philosophy
and the putting into practice were two distinctly different things.

Now with the world in the sorry state it's in, the kids are saying to
us, "Please, face reality with us, we can't wait any longer." And in
my opinion, they're absolutely correct; there is very little time left to
change our direction. It's not, as some educators think, merely a
case of acceding to a few demands and negotiating a few things. It's
much deeper, much deeper, than that. Some schools are responding by putting lots of things on paper. They say that they are in-
novating and trying all sorts of new scheduling methods. They're big
on open schools and all the latest gadgetry. But in reality, I'm afraid
much of the thinking of teachers and administrators is the same as it
was 10 years ago—same product with just new packaging. They are,
after all, the same people underneath. And in some cases, I'm afraid,
their feelings about kids are even worse than a few years ago because there is, now, a much greater polarization between kids and
adults. You see, there are many teachers who are quite frightened
by children. They are very much afraid of them; probably because
they don't really understand them. They equate the kid's appearance
as representing what that kid is as a human being. Not all teachers

do this, of course. There are a number of teachers who can accept students as persons. And where we have superior teacher-student relations, where we have wonderful things taking place in school, invariably, we will find a teacher who is himself an emotionally mature person. Only an emotionally sound person can create a healthy, humane atmosphere. The teacher need not be brilliant, just human. He doesn't advertise what he's doing as an "innovation," but he, himself, is the innovation. He's exciting, he's human, and what is more, he's socially relevant. He's the innovation. He makes marvelous things happen. And no labels can be put on those marvelous things. We just aren't getting enough of these kinds of teachers. Maybe there just isn't sufficient humanness to go around. Maybe, our training to become teachers and our whole process of socialization in America has dried up much of the humanness with which we were born. Who knows? One thing is for sure, things aren't looking too promising for the days ahead.

Suggestions for Further Study

1. What key issues are you able to identify from the selection?
2. Take any of these issues and do the following:

   (a) Determine the philosophical assumptions underlying the issue.
   (b) Try to discern in what direct or indirect way the issue seems to relate to students, classroom teachers.
   (c) In view of what you discovered above, what would you recommend as means for altering prevailing conditions to more optimally effect the teaching-learning processes in schools with which you are familiar?

3. Interview, on tape, one or more principals or other school officials in your local area (retired, neophyte, or experienced) about "school in the days ahead" and compare their views with Brian Joseph's.
4. Develop a panel of administrators, teachers, and students

from a nearby school to discuss the topic "School Days: 2001" and compare their views with Brian Joseph's.

5. Write an essay that synthesizes your examination of the selection, drawing from your efforts in any or all of the above.

Theme 2   School-Community Relations

American schools, hewn from the little red schoolhouses of the nineteenth century, have a tradition of often-stringent local influence and control, as contrasted with centrally governed systems common to France and many other countries. The once diverse, small, and rural American society has evolved in recent years into a relatively few, often ungovernable and enormous, population centers. The current question of community influence and control takes on new and extremely complicated dimensions. Whether local influence over school budgets, boards of education and educational policy continue to be possible, let alone effective, remains the basis for continuing controversy.

Helen Davis personifies this issue as she puts her values, emotions, and job directly on the line for "Lace Tablecloths and Silver Tea Service."

Selection 2   LACE TABLECLOTHS AND
              SILVER TEA SERVICE

Teacher: Helen Davis
Age: 28
Experience: 6 years, secondary

"It's obvious that the union is afraid of community control. They don't want to bargain with communities. They don't want to be held accountable by the community. Yes, mister, I'm a member of the union, and I feel that the union has done a great deal to advance the conditions of teachers, *but* when we, as professionals, become so unionized that we forget our mission to children, then I think we're shirking our duty as educators. That, sir, is why I'm telling you for the last time, let me enter the school building."

Helen Davis, a home-economics teacher in Metropolitan Junior High, tried, to no avail, to make her way through the line of teacher-pickets parading in front of the school. Later, she gained entrance by one of the side doors and walked quietly and nervously toward her classroom on the second floor.

"All that yelling by teachers out there in the street. Some example we're setting for the youngsters. Shocking!" Suddenly, the reality of what she was doing dawned on her. "Gads, I'm in the school, I'm a strikebreaker. Well, a person's got the right to take a stand for something, if he really believes in something. Sure, a lot of my teacher friends give lip service to the notion that they prefer going to work, and not being on the picket line. But, they're afraid of the consequences. Oh no, it isn't easy to buck the union."

Helen was pleased to find more than half of her students in attendance, and in her mind, the day was inspiring, in terms of classroom teaching.

18

That evening her good friend, Paul Jenner, visited her home.

"You shouldn't have done it, Helen. You never should have done it," Paul lamented. "You never should have crossed that picket line."

"Paul, it was a matter of conscience. You know as well as I do that there's a double standard in the schools of this city. That's what the strike is really all about. That, and little else."

"It's really more complex than that, Helen."

"No, Paul. It's really very simple. I've been in the system long enough to know that we have one set of standards for the white middle-class community and another for the blacks. I've worked on both sides of the fence in this city.

"In Oakhurst, the black section where I used to work, the parents didn't have any influence at all over what the teachers taught and said. No influence whatsoever over what happened to their child. Teachers taught when they felt like it and only if they felt like it. I've heard them say, 'I'll do just as much as I like, and no more.'

"One day, while in Oakhurst, one of the supervisors came to visit me. I had spent a lot of time painting the classroom, it was so dirty, and was struggling to get some home ec equipment into the school. We didn't have a set of measuring spoons, cheap as they are. Can you believe that?

"The girls and I had painted the cabinets. The girls brought in smocks and worked so hard. We had a cake sale and the paint was purchased from the profits. The place really had started to brighten up. It was even getting cheerful in that room. Well, when the supervisor dropped by, I asked her if she could expedite our getting the lace tablecloths that were in our order list—and also a silverplated tea service, which is really not too expensive. I had them in some of the other schools, in better neighborhoods. Well, Paul, she said to me, 'Miss Davis, don't you realize that these children do not have silver tea services or lace tablecloths at home? Why would you want to have them here? It's ridiculous! Oh no, we can't put such things in this type of school.' "

"How did you answer her?" Paul asked.

"I told her, 'even if they don't have these things in their homes, they need to know such things exist, how to use them, and perhaps, set their sights for such things, someday, if they wish!'

"Paul, we didn't have books, we didn't have paper, lined paper. Even the most basic properties for learning were not available. But now that I'm teaching in a classy, white, middle-class neighborhood, I see a store room that looks like a department store. You go in and get as many cups and saucers as you want. We have three sets of tea service and six tablecloths!

"Here, teachers are accountable to the white middle-class parents. We have community control in effect because when these parents are heard. And how they are heard. And because of this, don't even wait for a conference. They let the teachers have it, right at the PTA meeting. Their kids have got to show progress or the parents are heard. And how are they heard. And because of this, there is progress. There's more learning taking place because there's more teaching going on.

"And Paul, it can happen in the ghetto schools, too. But only if the teachers manage to change their attitudes and begin to hold out some hope. You know, I got very depressed when I was taking that graduate course last term. So many teachers there held no hope for their kids. The teacher, more than anyone, must have hope for the children. We have got to stop categorizing youngsters as 'poor' or 'deprived'—or 'middle class.' We must see them simply as children who need to learn—and for whom we're going to do all we can to help them to learn. What's wrong with lace tablecloths and silver tea service for all kids? What's the union doing about that?

Suggestions for Further Study

1. Would you have thought and acted differently if you were the teacher involved? Discuss.
2. What key issues relating to community influence can you identify in this section? Delineate specific questions, then conduct a thorough inquiry using appropriate research methodology and discuss your findings. What books and/or articles can you identify that buttress your arguments?
3. To what extent is community influence similar or different in schools with which you are familiar?

4. Discover and interview influential members of various segments of the community. Look for pertinent community studies and reports.

Annotated Bibliography

Brameld, Theodore. *Philosophies of Education in Cultural Perspective.* New York: The Dryden Press, 1965. A useful text for gaining an overview of various philosophies of education.

Cremin, Lawrence A. *The Transformation of the School: Progressivism in American Education, 1876–1957.* New York: Alfred A. Knopf, 1961. An exceptional text that traces the development of the progressive era and its impact upon American education.

De Carlo, Julia and Constant A. Madon. *Innovations in Education for the Seventies: Selected Readings.* New York: Behavioral Publications, 1973. A comprehensive anthology that focuses upon six major innovations of the seventies.

Dewey, John. *Democracy and Education.* New York: The Free Press, 1966. A classic work describing Dewey's philosophy of pragmatism in American education.

Kneller, George F. (ed.) *Foundations of Education.* New York: John Wiley and Sons, Inc., 1971. A book of readings that gives an excellent overview of the foundations area.

Morris, Van Cleve. *Existentialism in Education.* New York: Harper and Row, 1966. An in-depth discussion of the existentialist philosophy in American education.

Phenix, Philip H. *Philosophy of Education.* New York: Henry Holt and Company, 1958. Presents sketches by noted authors of some contemporary viewpoints on education.

Section II TODAY'S STUDENT

There are a tremendous variety of forces impinging on today's student. It is, therefore, quite difficult to find a central focus or unifying point around which one can rally the masses of data that have been accumulated in various theoretical and empirical studies regarding American students. We focus on the *development of the student's self* as the locus or central theme of this essay. It will then be possible to separately examine particular developmental factors: physical, intellectual, social, and emotional qualities of students and perhaps more clearly grasp the connection between these factors in relation to development of the student's self-concept. It also becomes possible to examine the effects of other variables peculiar to society surrounding the student. These considerations include the influence of technology and communication, contemporary alienation and loneliness, drug usage, new morality codes, more permissive sexual relations, and prevailing youth-employment patterns. All of these social forces most certainly affect the development of students as well. The first group of variables are delineated as *developmental* because they develop over an extended period of time. The latter group are termed *external-randomized* because they occur outside of the student and are uneven in nature, receiving varying degrees of emphasis at different periods, depending upon the vagaries of society at any given time. A thorough understanding of developmental and external-randomized factors as they affect students should prove most useful to teachers. Many of the changes transpiring in a child occur according to a fairly well-

23

regulated schedule and knowledge of these changes afford parents and teachers a useful blueprint of what can be expected at various stages in a child's development. External-randomized variables are, by definition, less predictable.

The teacher is beset with having to interpret literally hundreds of signals set forth by students regarding their personality and needs at any given moment. To the untrained observer, they may remain unnoticed and uninterpreted. However, the teacher who has a background in developmental psychology from which to operate is able to organize these multifarious signals in ways that can be meaningful in helping individual youngsters. The trained teacher can often proceed to initiate a realistic diagnosis of each child's strengths and weaknesses and render valid teaching approaches and treatments. The bits of data can be assembled into a case study.

Stated simply, the case study provides a method of assembling and organizing various data about a student so that a holistic understanding and an accurate diagnosis can be rendered and a sound plan of help formulated.

Following is a case study checklist. This checklist serves the purpose of convening the innumerable bits of data that bear upon the development of a student. The checklist is adapted in part from a case study outline by John A. Demming.[1] Some of the items are followed by pages and/or figure numbers. These refer to specific material that is more extensively developed within this chapter. Applying this checklist to a particular student should prove an invaluable experience.

A CASE STUDY CHECKLIST

☐ **A.** Basic Data
  ☐ Student's name.
  ☐ Age.
  ☐ Appearance.

[1] *John A. Demming. "Case Study Outline,"* Readings in Guidance (*ed. by L. D. Crow and A. Crow) pp. 283–285, New York: David McKay Co., Inc. 1962.*

☐ School and grade level.

☐ Type of school program (major courses, curriculum, and grouping).

☐ **B.** The Problem

    ☐ Brief description of problems or special conditions bearing upon the student at the time of this study.

    ☐ Include observation reports and limits of this study.

☐ **C.** Family and Background

    ☐ Parents' or guardians' name and age. Same for siblings.

    ☐ Occupational history of key family members.

    ☐ Place of residence, description of neighborhood, house, surroundings, and sleeping and study arrangements.

    ☐ Socioeconomic circumstances.

    ☐ Physical health of various family members.

    ☐ Educational background of family members.

    ☐ Special aptitudes, interests, and achievements of various members of family.

    ☐ Attitudes of various members toward each other, but particularly effects of these attitudes toward the student under study.

    ☐ Estimate of emotional adjustment of various family members.

☐ **D.** Other members of the household

    ☐ Considerations of similar factors listed under C, above.

☐ **E.** The Community

    ☐ Describe the character of the community in which student lives.

    ☐ Describe the character of the community in which student lived.

    ☐ Describe the immediate neighborhood.

    ☐ Describe the immediate neighbors in terms of socioeconomic factors and special traits.

☐ **F.** Physical Development of the Student (see Gesell, Figure 1, p. 29).

    ☐ Birth history.

    ☐ Early patterns of development (such as bowel habits, walking, and use of language).

- ☐ General health at present.
- ☐ Eating habits.
- ☐ Height and weight.
- ☐ General appearance (hair color, complexion, body carriage, and so on).
- ☐ Overall estimate of physical condition (see McCandless, p. 34).
- ☐ **G.** Psychosocial development of the student (see Erikson, Figure 2, p. 35).
  - ☐ Standardized test data (achievement, aptitude, interest).
  - ☐ Cognitive development (see Piaget, Figure 5, p. 44).
  - ☐ Academic achievement record.
  - ☐ Personal achievements (p. 41).
  - ☐ Estimate of intellectual development (p. 43).
  - ☐ Completion of appropriate developmental tasks (see Havighurst, Figure 4, p. 40).
  - ☐ Peer relations, in and out of school.
  - ☐ Relationships with adults.
  - ☐ Social and moral code (p. 53).
  - ☐ Sex role identification (p. 36).
  - ☐ Sense of personal identity (see Erikson, Figure 2, p. 35).
  - ☐ Social graces.
  - ☐ Leadership qualities.
  - ☐ Relationship with authority figures (parents, teachers).
  - ☐ Cooperation.
  - ☐ Level of self-concept development (see p. 46).
  - ☐ Ideals and values.
  - ☐ Need system (see Maslow, Figure 3, p. 37).
  - ☐ Areas of conflict.
  - ☐ Maturity level of interests.
  - ☐ Sense of autonomy (p. 35).
  - ☐ Degree of alienation (p. 55).
  - ☐ Dependency upon external substances such as drugs (p. 52).
  - ☐ Curiosity.
  - ☐ Persistence.

- ☐ Capacity to love.
- ☐ Capacity to be loved.
- ☐ Other factors.
☐ **H.** The Interface Between Developmental and External-
Randomized Variables (see p. 57)
☐ **I.** Evaluation and Recommendations
- ☐ Review all the data, observe for recurring themes and prevailing conditions, with special consideration as to how these factors bear upon the problems or conditions described in B. How do these data reflect upon the student's emerging sense of self?
- ☐ Develop and enumerate various strategies and/or courses of action toward enhancing the student's personal development.

DEVELOPMENTAL FACTORS AS THEY RELATE TO STUDENT'S SELF-CONCEPT

Patterns of normal development give us information about what to expect from the majority of youngsters. Descriptive material, studies, and positions from the more tenable and widely held theoretical positions regarding "normal" development ensue.

Physical, Motor and Language Development

Evidence from Gesell (1940, 1946, 1956) and McCandless (1967) supports the idea of specific physical, motor, and language patterns occurring at given times in the growth cycle. The data clearly indicate a relationship between a child's physical development and the *development of self.* Atypical growth patterns are likely to affect the child's self-concept. This knowledge is useful to the teacher on two levels. First, she can use the normative data to establish a model of normal physical development. Secondly, she can feed into the model the data and the signals that she is receiving from her students, thus identifying youngsters who are atypical and who may need special attention. For example, with a youngster of a given age who is overweight or underweight, too short or too tall, or who lacks adequate motor coordination, a study can be initiated to ascertain the likely effects of his atypical condition on his personal development. The teacher can then develop a plan that, although it cannot correct the physical problem, may alleviate some of the negative effects that result from it. It has been found, for example, that boys with small genital organs can be guided through the difficult adolescent years with additional counseling, and that both early and late maturing boys and girls can be helped by providing special opportunities for social interaction with youngsters at grade levels either above or below their own.

Knowledge of physical development can, therefore, enable the teacher to develop effective strategies for dealing with each child individually and to enhance the child's opportunities for success.

The Gesell Institute Studies

The research of Gesell and Thompson (1940) can be particularly useful to both parents and teachers for planning and carrying out effective child-development practices (see Figure 1). They studied children from 107 families from birth to age five. Five different types of records were kept on each child.

1. A stenographic record was taken of responses to standardized situations.

2. A behavior day record was kept, recording the times of day that a baby usually slept, ate, and played, for example.

3. A record was kept of the child's behavior at home as it pertained to his developing skills.

4. Physical measurements were taken to determine typical size, weight, and mental development at different ages.

5. A prenatal history and record of early development was taken in order to exclude children with physical abnormalities.

Changes were recorded in growth patterns in 50 percent or more of the population sample and normative descriptions for various intervals of 4, 12, and 20 weeks, for example, through the first 5 years of life (see Figure 1). Gesell and Ilg (1946) conducted similar studies and descriptive material regarding children 5 through 10 years of age. In still another study, Gesell, Ilg, and Ames (1956), continued the research on youngsters 11 through 16.

☐ *Figure 1*   **Gesell's Developmental Stages**

Four weeks. While the infant can hold his head at mid-position, he is more likely to turn it to one side or the other. He does not fix his eyes on objects unless they are in his direct line of vision. He cannot grasp a rattle when it is given to him. No vocalization or prelanguage appears, only small throaty noises.

Twelve weeks. The child still holds his head to one side or the other. He begins to track objects as they are moved from side to side within the line of his vision. He can grasp the rattle and hold it for a period of time. Vocalization and prelanguage are still not present.

Twenty weeks. The infant can hold his head erect. When put in a standing position, he can support his own weight momentarily. He grasps the rattle quickly and brings it to his mouth. He turns his head to the sound of a voice or bell but not necessarily to the correct side.

Twenty-eight weeks. He brings his head forward and tries to sit up. He can support his own weight in a standing position for more than a moment. He can transfer an object from one hand to the other. Toys are frequently placed in his mouth

Thirty-six weeks. If supported on each side, he can stand on his toes. He can grasp objects with either hand and does not show hand preference. He can say a short syllable such as "da" or "da da" or "ma ma."

Forty-four weeks. The child is able to creep. With some help he can pull himself to a standing position. He can easily move from the prone position to a sitting position.

Figure 1 (continued)

He can copy movements after the examiner, such as marking a paper with a crayon. He can grasp an object and release it on command from the examiner.

Fifty-two weeks. The child can walk with the support of one or both hands. He can hold an object in one hand while grasping for another object with the other. He looks at a mirror reflection of himself and talks to it using two or more words.

Eighteen months. The child walks with a stiff gait; he can seat himself on a child's chair, creep downstairs and walk upstairs. He can roll a ball, turn the pages of a book, pile two or three blocks vertically, and has about a 10-word speaking vocabulary. He is just beginning to gain some control of his sphincter muscles.

Twenty-four months. The child can run and kick a ball. He can cut paper with scissors, build a tower of six blocks, and identify many objects in pictures. He is beginning to use the words "I," "you," and "me" but has difficulty with the "I-you" concept. He begins to use the negative form and can distinguish that a knife, for example, is not a fork. He helps to dress and undress himself. Though toilet training is not complete, he can usually sleep without wetting the bed. At mealtimes he may be a great dawdler.

Three years. At three years the child's attention span is extended so that he can keep at an activity much longer. He enjoys repeating the same act, such as playing with a puzzle box or a set of blocks. He can fold a piece of paper lengthwise and crosswise but not diagonally. He uses sentences effectively and can execute fairly complex commands. He tends to be more cooperative than at two and takes suggestions more readily. He is more interested in playing with other children.

Five years. The child is more self assured and has a capacity for friendship. He can skip easily, do simple dances, brush his teeth, and comb his hair. He can draw a man fairly well and can rearrange the two diagonally cut halves

Figure 1 (continued)

of a card to form a rectangle. He knows his name and address. He can tell his left hand from his right but not on other people. He begins to connect function and object, such as "a bicycle is to ride."

Six years. At this age the child is very active. Tree climbing and wrestling are popular. Six-year-olds are big eaters, although their table manners and control of utensils may be poor. Boys tend to resist bathing. At school these children like to associate physical activity with subject matter. They may tend to take things that don't belong to them. They may also be indulging in some sex play and exhibitionism.

Seven years. The seven-year-old can read a clock and may be able to tie his shoelaces. He tends to be a perfectionist about his school work. He is more cooperative than he was a year earlier and likes a close personal friendship with his teacher. Boys may withdraw from unpleasant situations rather than charging into physical combat as they did at six years. He may be developing minor love affairs with girls his age.

Eight years. He tends to be more reckless than he was a year earlier, and bicycle accidents are more common. Girls are interested in finding out about the origins of babies and about menstruation. Both boys and girls enjoy school with the focus shifting from the teacher to other students. A seven-year-old's writing of sentences is beginning to be fairly uniform in spacing and slant and he draws human figures with some sense of proportion.

Nine years. The nine-year-old tends to be self-motivated. He shows less frustration at completing difficult tasks. He enjoys reading and may be ready to practice a musical instrument. He may, however, dislike arithmetic. He may tend toward excessive physical activity and require time to regain his energies. Eating is more temperate. Boys may tend to restrict themselves to a single close friend while girls often have larger friendship groups.

Figure 1   (continued)

Ten years. Ten-year-olds seem less tense than a year earlier. There is less rivalry with siblings, parents, and friends. Boys and girls tend to have separate activities. Boys prefer outdoor games. Unlike earlier years, the father may be especially important to these children. At school they expect their teachers to be friendly to every student, not just themselves. They love to memorize, yet have difficulty connecting two or more facts. Girls are already showing signs of sexual maturity and may have a slight projection of their nipples and a little downy pubic hair. Boys may be learning dirty jokes and "four letter Anglo-Saxon words."

Eleven years. The 11-year-old tends to be rebellious and quarrelsome with parents and teachers. They may be very critical of school policy. In relationships with teachers they can be treated firmly but they expect fairness in all their dealings. Conflicts arise from differences in values between parents and those of the peer group. Physically, girls are showing a conelike breast development and some pubic hair. Some boys have downy pubic hair and larger genitals Most boys have experienced erections; some have masturbated. Cognitively, they are more fact than conceptually oriented. They are motivated by school and competition and see school as a place to meet friends.

Twelve years. The rebelliousness of the previous year tends to be less intense, and 12-year-olds are more friendly and cooperative. Boys are more interested in school and enjoy reading science fiction. They enjoy sports but may tend to overexert themselves. Girls enjoy the social aspects of school and take an interest in home economics. Girls will probably menstruate before age 13. Boys know about ejaculation, but some still have not experienced it.

Thirteen years. The 13-year-old tends to do more thinking about school, his teacher, and his parents. He is becoming more discriminate in his choice of friends. Emotionally, he seems to be better controlled yet may be prone to moodiness at times. At school he is less boisterous, but

Figure 1   (continued)

may at the same time be very critical of the school principal. Boys are beginning to show darkened hair over the
lip. Girls are filling out in the breasts and growing taller.

Fourteen years. At 14 he is more outgoing and friendly
than at 13. He enjoys being with friends and tends to associate with others in groups. He enjoys school organizations and likes to actively participate in them. Girls have
now developed enough to look like young adults. Boys
have experienced ejaculation and nocturnal emissions.
Their voices are deepened and they have dense pubic
hair. Some youngsters have tried smoking and discuss
drinking.

Fifteen years. Fifteen-year-olds seek independence and
privacy. They are hesitant to discuss personal problems
with parents or teachers. Boys are thinking about careers
although not often of marriage because they do not want to
be tied down. They enjoy working for others and testing
their abilities in the "real world." Girls, on the other hand,
are contemplating marriage. Boys and girls enjoy being in
groups and participating in discussions of various kinds.
Most boys and girls have experimented with smoking.

Sixteen years. The 16-year-old seems to be more self assured, less emotionally insecure about himself. He is less
egotistical in his thinking and can begin to see others'
points of view. There is less tension with parents and
teachers and he has better control of his emotions. Boys
tend to seek friends on the basis of mutual interests. Girls
are more selective in their choice of a few close friends.
For boys, masturbation is the most common form of ejaculation, with an increasing frequency of nocturnal emissions. Kissing and petting between boys and girls are ways
of showing affection. Boys and girls are interested in their
future career, education, and marriage, although marriage
tends to be more of interest to girls than boys. Both want
to succeed academically and fulfill their own potential. □

Types of Physical Changes: McCandless

McCandless (1967) has identified various types of physical changes that transpire in the human organism. The purpose in delineating these changes here is simply to underscore the point that the youngsters are involved in a very *powerful* physical *change process* in their childhood and adolescent years . . . the years in school. The types of change identified by McCandless include the following:

1. *Changes in kind.* The zygote is very different in kind from the sperm and egg that make it up; pubic hair is very different from childhood down.

2. *Changes in number.* At five, the child has 48 to 52 teeth in one stage of development or another; by adolescence 20 deciduous (baby) teeth have been lost; by adolescence one or more third molars (the wisdom teeth) have often been lost; and by old age it is common to have lost all one's teeth.

3. *Changes in size.* The child steadily increases in height to 18 years of age or so, but in middle and old age height actually decreases; the primary sex characteristics develop very slowly during childhood but increase dramatically in size before, during, and for a time after puberty.

4. *Changes in shape.* The proportions of the adolescent are very different from those of the baby; the chest becomes broader and flatter during childhood, more circular again after middle age.

5. *Changes in position.* Elbows and knees at first project outward from the sides of the body. Later the knees rotate toward the front, the elbows toward the back; feet move from paralleling the axis of the lower leg toward the perpendicular.

6. *Changes in pigmentation.* Hair usually grows darker during childhood and ordinarily grays in middle and old age; skin darkens in middle age.

7. *Changes in texture.* Muscles harden, particularly for males during and after adolescence; in middle and old age bones become brittle and skin loses its elasticity.

8. *Changes in function.* The mouth becomes less of an in-

strument of sucking and more of an instrument of biting, chewing, and vocalizing; the sphincter muscles come under voluntary control; legs are used for walking. The penis acquires the function of ejaculation.

Social and Emotional Development

Although less obvious and measurable than the physical aspects, the social and emotional variables can also be viewed as developmental with certain patterns occurring within given time periods. The theories of Erik Erikson, Abraham Maslow, and Robert Havighurst will be presented to illustrate the developmental nature of social and emotional growth. We have highlighted the major tenets of their important work in this area.

Erik Erikson.   In the socialization process, Erikson (1956) has identified eight progressive stages. Each stage is regarded as a "psychosocial crisis" which must be resolved before the next stage can be successfully negotiated (see Figure 2).

Erikson's theory delineates the developmental qualities inherent in social and emotional growth, and his theory provides a model for examining students. For instance, if a parent knows that his child needs to develop a degree of trust, autonomy, and initiative before he starts school, then perhaps sufficient experiences can be offered prior to school entry to achieve these ends. Idealistically, perhaps, if the teacher recognized that a child needs to develop a modicum of industry and sufficient personal identity, she, too, can structure certain affective experiences in order to achieve these objectives.

□ *Figure 2   Erikson's Psychosocial Stages*

Learning Trust versus Mistrust (0–2 years). The child who is well handled and loved learns trust and security. If he is badly handled, he becomes insecure and mistrustful.

Learning Autonomy versus Shame (18 months–4 years). During this period the child learns toilet training and becomes proud of his newfound control. A child who has dif-

Figure 2   (continued)

ficulty at this stage tends to be ashamed and develops doubts over the control of his body function.

Learning Initiative versus Guilt (3½–5 years). The child at this stage begins to develop his skills in play activities and learns to cooperate with others. Lack of success can make him fearful and overly dependent on adults.

Industry versus Inferiority (school age). Here the child learns to master the skills needed to succeed in school: basic school subjects, sports, and self-discipline. He develops a sense of industry toward his work. The child who cannot negotiate this stage successfully tends to feel inferior and experiences guilt feelings.

Learning Identity versus Identity Diffusion (adolescence). The psychosocial crisis at this stage deals with the question "Who am I?" At the beginning of this period the child acquires self-certainty and anticipates achievement. In later adolescence, clear sexual identity is established. The unsuccessful person at this stage experiences self-doubt, identity diffusion, and can become paralyzed by feelings of inferiority.

Learning Intimacy versus Isolation (young adult). Successful persons are able to achieve a sense of true intimacy leading to courtship and marriage. Not mastering this crisis may lead to isolation and more self-doubt and inferiority.

Learning Generativity versus Self-Absorption (adult). This psychosocial crisis deals with generativity in marriage and parenthood. It also refers to working productively and creatively. Failure to achieve these goals leads to self-absorption.

Integrity versus Despair (mature adult). If the other seven psychosocial crises have been resolved successfully, the mature adult develops integrity. He trusts, is independent, works hard and has found a well-defined role in life. He has a healthy self-concept and is proud of what he creates.

Figure 2   (continued)
If, on the other hand, one or more of the previous psycho-social crises have not been resolved, he may view his life with disgust and despair. □

Abraham Maslow.   Basic human needs and the attainment of these needs are discussed by Maslow (1954). He holds that basic goals are related to each other, arranged in a hierarchy of prepotency (see Figure 3). This means that the most prepotent goal will monopolize consciousness and will tend itself to organize the recruitment of the various capacities of the organism. The less-prepotent needs are minimized, even forgotten or denied. When a need is fairly well satisfied, the next prepotent (higher) need emerges to dominate the conscious life and to serve as the center of organization of behavior since gratified needs are not active motivators.

Thus, man is a perpetually wanting animal. Ordinarily the satisfaction of these wants is not altogether mutually exclusive but only tends to be. The average member of our society is most often partially satisfied and partially unsatisfied in all of his wants. The hierarchy principle is usually empirically observed in terms of increasing percentages of nonsatisfaction as we go up the hierarchy.

□ *Figure 3   **Maslow's Hierarchy of Human Needs***

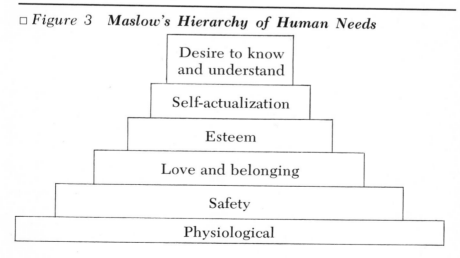

Figure 3   (continued)

Physiological Needs. These needs are usually taken as the starting point for Maslow's (1943) theory. He refers to them as the most prepotent of all needs. In other words, a person lacking food, for example, would place this need above those of safety, love, and esteem, pushing the latter into the background. Gratification of physiological needs releases the organism from the domination of those needs and frees him to pursue the next-higher need. What previously dominated the individual toward physiological needs is now directed toward a new and unsatisfied goal.

Safety Needs. If the organism has satisfied his physiological needs, then the safety need becomes the dominating force in the person's behavior. For the very young child the safety need expresses itself in the need for some kind of undisrupted routine or rhythm. Inconsistency and unfairness tend to upset the child and make him anxious and threatened. Also, speaking harshly, handling him roughly, or actual physical punishment can throw him into total panic and terror. Most healthy adults have met their safety needs, however, some neurotic persons still behave as though their safety needs were not gratified. Some tend to be compulsive-obsessive trying frantically to organize and stabilize their worlds. Others tend to avoid everything unfamiliar and strange and shy away from situations that they feel they cannot handle. If something unexpected does occur, it tends to provoke the same reaction of panic and terror.

Love Needs. When both physiological and safety needs are met there will emerge the love, affection, and belongingness needs. The absence of friends is keenly felt as is the need for a sweetheart, wife, or children. The individual longs for a place in his group and will strive to achieve this goal. The love need, while closely related to sexual satisfaction, is more complex and is not only sexual but is determined by the need for giving and receiving.

Esteem Needs. With few exceptions all persons desire self-respect or self-esteem. These persons are usually satisfied

Figure 3 (continued

through achievement, independence, and freedom. There is also a strong desire for reputation, prestige, recognition, and appreciation. Thwarting of these needs leads to inferiority, weakness, and helplessness.

Need for Self-Actualization. After fulfillment of all previous needs, there is the need to achieve one's full potential, called self-actualization. People at this level are satisfied and show their creativeness in expressing themselves through a varity of activities. Great individuality is exhibited by persons at this level of development.

Desire to Know and Understand. Closely related to the basic affective needs is the cognitive need to know and understand. Intelligent people have a very strong drive in this area. Less intelligent people were not included, since data are lacking for this group. The desire to know and understand is closely related to the other basic needs and is a function of the total personality. □

Reversals of the average order of the hierarchy are sometimes observed. An individual may permanently lose the higher wants in the hierarchy under special conditions. There are not only ordinary multiple motivations for usual behavior but, in addition, many detriments other than motives.

If we accept Maslow's premise of a hierarchy of needs, then it is imperative that teachers, after ascertaining that physiological and safety needs of the student are met, should incorporate opportunities to meet the love, belonging, and esteem needs of the student. In order for a student to develop into a self-actualizing person, the teacher must take an active part in having the child develop the feelings of self-worth. The student should be experiencing sufficient success in the cognitive and affective areas so that he will develop a positive self-concept and will feel adequate in himself as a person.

Robert Havighurst. Havighurst's main contribution was to demonstrate the necessity for an individual to complete one developmental task *before* he can properly proceed to the next level. He points out that a particular developmental task can be undertaken only after one or more of the following conditions has been met:

1.   Physical maturation has reached a point sufficient to endow the person with the physical resources necessary for the task.

2.   The society expects certain behavior forms.

3.   The personal values, aspirations, and psychological competence of the individual make it possible or necessary for the individual to enter into an activity.

For example, a youngster in early childhood can learn to take in solid foods only when physically ready; in middle and late childhood, a youngster can master the concepts required for daily living (conscience, morality, and values) only after he has mastered preceding concepts, such as a belief in "right" and "wrong" (see Figure 4).

The concept of the developmental task is helpful in thinking about the process of education for two reasons. First, it helps in discovering and stating purposes of education in the schools. Education may be conceived as the effort of society, through the school, to help the individual achieve, certain of his developmental tasks. The second use of the concept is in the timing of educational efforts. Havighurst states:

> When the body is ripe, and the society requires, and the self is ready to achieve a certain task, the teachable moment has come. Efforts at teaching which would have been largely wasted if they had come earlier, give gratifying results when they come at the teachable moment, when the task should be learned.
>
> (Havighurst, 1954, p. 7)

□ *Figure 4   **Havighurst's Developmental Tasks***

Age Span	Appropriate Tasks
Birth through early childhood	Learning to take solid foods Learning to walk Learning to talk

Figure 4   (*continued*)

Age Span	Appropriate Tasks
	Learning to control bodily elimination
	Learning sex differences and appropriate standards for modesty
	Learning to make realistic emotional adjustments to family members and others
	Forming elementary concepts of physical and social reality
	Developing the concept of "right" and "wrong" and acquiring conscience
Middle and late childhood	Developing necessary physical skills for play and games
	Acquiring a wholesome concept of self
	Developing social skills in dealing with peers
	Further developing of appropriate sex and social roles
	Developing the "three Rs"
	Mastering the concepts required for daily living to include conscience, morality, and values
	Developing personal independence
Adolescence	Acquiring wholesome attitudes toward self and others
	Developing advanced skills necessary for more complex games
	Acquiring appropriate masculine and feminine roles
	Developing appropriate social skills
	Developing emotional and social independence from parents and others
	Determining and preparing for a vocational role

Figure 4   (continued)

Age Span	Appropriate Tasks
	Acquiring intellectual skills
	Preparing for marriage and family role
	Developing civic and social competencies and ethical values
Early adulthood	Selecting and accepting an occupation
	Selecting a mate
	Making necessary adjustments to live with marriage partner
	Preparing for and managing a family and home
	Assuming civic responsibility
	Locating a congenial social group
Middle years of adulthood	Assuming economic, civic and social responsibility
	Assisting offspring to make necessary social and economic adjustments for a satisfying relationship in the social spectrum
	Developing satisfying avocations and leisure time activities
	Developing a satisfying relationship with one's own spouse
	Making necessary changes to accept the physiological changes of middle age
	Making necessary adjustments to parents, relatives, and others
Late adulthood	Adjusting to decreasing strength and health problems associated with aging
	Adjusting to retirement and reduced income
	Adjusting to increased leisure time

Figure 4   (continued)

Age Span   *Appropriate Tasks*

Establishing satisfactory adjustments
to changing living arrangements
Establishing an explicit affiliation
with one's age group
Adjusting to the death of spouse □

Intellectual Development

We have noted the developmental nature of the physical, social, and emotional variables as they relate to the student.
Jean Piaget (1958) has done extremely important work regarding the cognitive development of children. Throughout his
works he reiterates that cognitive intellectual changes are the
result of the developmental process. Piaget divides intellectual development into four periods or stages. He notes that
cognitive development flows along from one stage to another,
not in discrete steps. The age spans suggested for each phase
are normative and only denote the approximate time when
most children are expected to demonstrate the characteristic
intellectual behavior of that phase. According to Piaget, although each child *must* pass through each stage he does so at
his own *individual rate.* This accounts for the bright child who
passes rapidly through the stages and also for the slow child
who moves laboriously through each stage (Figure 5).

Comprehension of Piaget's theory is indispensable to the
teacher attempting to better understand the cognitive development of his students. According to Piaget, the child in the elementary grades must be an active participant in the learning
process. He needs to discover relationships through the use of
concrete materials in order to form concepts. He is not able to
accept the abstractions that only verbal learning will give because he has not attained that stage in his development. In the
junior high and senior high school, more of his learning can be
achieved through the use of verbalization and may be on an

abstract level because the student will have attained a greater capacity for cognitive learning.

One observes from Piaget's schema that cognitive growth, like physical, social, and emotional growth, can also be considered developmental in nature. It proceeds from the simple to the complex. It should be noted that significant changes in the *quality of thinking* occur in adolescence, interconnecting physical, social, and emotional changes. While the child is experiencing the physical changes that come with the onset of puberty, he is, at the same time, searching for his identity. He, emotionally and cognitively, is becoming detached from the concrete world and can begin to think in abstract terms. There is obviously an intricate orchestration of various forces at work in the development of a child and later a student.

☐ *Figure 5* **Piaget's Phases of Cognitive Development**

Sensorimotor Stage (0–2 years). The child depends primarily on sensorimotor and body-motor experience. He is dependent on his body for communication and self-expression. During this period he learns to coordinate perceptual and motor functions and to utilize certain elementary schemata (generalized behavior patterns or dispositions) for dealing with objects external to himself. He arrives at the knowledge that such objects exist even when he cannot see or touch them or otherwise be aware of them. The major developmental task of this period is the coordination of actions or motor activities into a tenuous whole new organism; in other words, he must find himself an active part of his environment within the limits of his immediate experience.

Preoperational Thought (2–7 years). Piaget describes this period as a transaction between life patterns of purely self-satisfying behavior and rudimentary socialized behavior. The child's life is one of continual investigation. He discovers new symbols to use in communication with self and others. These symbols are primarily self-referenced. Even though the child and adult employ the same lan-

Figure 5   (continued)

guage, they do not necessarily have a mutual framework of communication. The child knows the world only as he sees it, based on his previous experience. This limited view leads to his assumption that everyone thinks as he does and understands him, without the necessity of his having to convey his thoughts and feelings. Assimilation is the paramount role of the child here. The child perceives the world from an egocentric vantage point. Through language he not only repeats sensorimotor developmental history but replaces it—speech becomes the conveyor of meaning. He can verbally express desire, experience, and thought without having to act them out. This is a necessary step before he can learn to generalize and to comprehend objective concepts. Imitation and symbolic imitations of others is a spontaneous process at this stage. Play is also important. Still relying on previous experience with sequential relationships, the child interprets experience in terms of subjective proximity: what occurs in proximity to something else has some relationship. *Animism* is also a characteristic at this time. There are two essential phenomenological characteristics of this period:

1. Reasoning is based on subjective judgement regardless of their objective logic.
2. The child tends to experience either the qualitative or quantitative aspect but does not experience both at once or any connective relationship between the two notions. He cannot yet merge concepts of objects, space, and causality into temporal interrelationships with a time concept.

This preconcept of causality is marked by two tendencies:

1. The tendency to bestow power onto objects. This derives from the fact that he no longer considers all actions as emanating from the self. There is basically a failure in his thinking to differentiate between his own actions and those of the object.
2. The tendency to invest a model with unusual power that gives rise to identification.

Figure 5   (continued)

Stage of Concrete Operations (7–11 years). An operation is a type of action carried out by manipulation of objects, or internally. An internalized operation is a means of getting data about the real world into the mind and there transforming them so that they can be organized and used selectively in the solution of problems. At this stage, the concept of reversibility becomes clear. The child can use environmental clues to make adjustments and can think through to a desired solution rather than using actual trial and error. The conservation principle now can be understood. A child does not enter this stage abruptly; he still does preconceptual thinking, but in general he can reason successfully about things that now are or have been concretely present before him. He must have the ability to make sharp distinctions between related properties such as true distance and distance as it appears to be, weight, and density. He can deal mentally with the properties of the immediately present world.

Stage of Formal Operations (12–15 years). This stage involves the appearance of formal operations. The child can reason about a possibility not here and now actually present. He can use symbols or abstract ideas systematically. Relations involving more than one variable can be comprehended. He can make comparisons and deductions accurately from information not concretely presented. The most significant change in the child's thinking is that he moves from the concrete world into the world of ideas. He is no longer tied to the real world. □

DEVELOPMENTAL FACTORS AND SELF-CONCEPT

Through the study of atypical youngsters, a physical, social, emotional, or intellectual variable often becomes more visible. The studies reviewed below deal with both typical and atypical cases and highlight the connection between developmental variables and the development of self-concept.

The Relationship Between Physical Development and the
Development of Self-Concept

Several studies graphically indicate the connection between physical growth and the development of self. Schonfeld (1950) studied 256 boys who had expressed concern over their physical development. He found that inadequate masculine physique, small sex organs, or a deficiency of secondary sex characteristics can cause considerable concern and result in serious personality conflicts or psychomotor complaints. A study by Angelino and Mech (1956) reported similar concern about physical development for girls. Worry most often centered on the effects of deviant height and weight development on their social and emotional life.

Jones (1949) conducted a series of studies on the relationships between early and late maturation of girls and boys and social adjustment. A sample of 20 percent of early maturers and 20 percent of late maturers based upon skeletal X-rays were chosen from a public school in California. He found that the early maturing girl became very conspicuous and was handicapped in physical activities involving running and jumping. She was quite naturally interested in boys and was forced to associate with older adolescents. In her own age group she was ill at ease and frustrated. Late-maturing girls, on the other hand, tended to be superior in traits related to personal appearance and attractiveness, in buoyance, poise, and cheerfulness, and also in sociability, leadership, and prestige. In their relationships with the opposite sex, the late-maturing girls tended to be more nearly in step with boys of their own age group resulting from the lag in the latter's development.

For boys the reverse pattern was found. Early-maturing boys with the traits of strength and athletic ability had prestige with their own sex. They were able to date girls of their own age group and were shown to be quite successful socially.

Sex differences also affect self-concept. Reese (1961) studied fourth-, sixth-, and eighth-grade youngsters in upstate New York. He found that girls usually reported higher self-esteem scores than boys. Both boys and girls who "liked themselves" also liked others.

Clearly then, patterns of physical growth do significantly affect the psychological development of a person. Even the obvious factors of height, weight, and body build play a role in social and emotional development.

The Relationship Between Social and Emotional Development and the Development of Self-Concept

Numerous studies have been conducted showing the obvious connection between a youngster's social and emotional development and his development as a person. We have chosen several to illustrate the character of this relationship.

In separate studies of school-age children, Ausubel (1952) and Russell (1953) found that elementary school youngsters have difficulty in judging themselves accurately. They tend to overestimate their good qualities and underestimate their socially disapproved ones. As the child grows older, his concepts of himself are clarified through the discovery of new qualities and potentialities.

The Incomplete Sentences Test was used by Crandall and Bellugi (1954) to rate the self-concept of college juniors and seniors. They reported that a positive self-concept is related to satisfactory social and behavioral adjustment.

In middle childhood and early adolescence, teacher and peer appraisal play a significant part in the child's self-appraisal. Sears and Sherman (1964) found that self-esteem develops when self-appraisals are consistent with the appraisal of significant others, i.e. teachers and peers. In cases where teacher appraisal was either lacking or inconsistent, youngsters tended to feel insecure and unsure of themselves.

A discussion of the relationship between social and emotional development, and the development of self-concept should include some mention of the influence of one's culture or subculture. Disadvantaged youngsters, particularly blacks, have often been reported to have inadequate views of themselves. Separate studies by both Kvaraceus (1965) and Deutsch (1962) noted that the black child's basic self-concept is shaped by the appraisal of society regarding his status and is acquired during the preschool years.

Long and Henderson (1966) matched 72 black and white children entering a rural school in the South according to age, grade, and sex and found that black children had a lower self-esteem than whites. Along with physical characteristics, then, social, emotional, and even cultural factors contribute an important part to the child's development of selfhood.

The Relationship Between Intellectual Development and the Development of Self-Concept

One of the most fascinating studies relating to intellectual achievement was conducted by Rosenthal and Jacobson (1968). Operating on the assumption that teacher expectation plays an important role in student performance, the researchers randomly selected 20 percent of the children in an elementary school in California and *misinformed* their teachers that they could expect significant intellectual growth spurts in the children selected on the basis of an artificial test. A pretest-posttest procedure measuring scholastic ability was utilized with the selected children and showed significantly greater gains in scholastic ability test scores than did the non-selected children in the school. Actual score changes ranged from −6 to +69 with a total average gain for all youngsters selected in grades one through six of 12.22. The point of this study was to check the effects of teacher expectancy on student development. It served to demonstrate that when a teacher expected a student to do well, the student fulfilled the teacher's prophecy. This is known as the "self-fulfilling prophecy" effect.

Bereiter and Engelmann (1966) developed a special intensive program for 15 black children, ages four to five and one-half years. After one year of concentrated instruction in basic language skills, reading and arithmetic, they were able to raise the scholastic-ability test score of the children from below average to average and raise the reading and arithmetic scores to the first and second grade, respectively.

Other researchers, however, did not achieve the same degree of success. Weikart (1967) in the Perry Preschool Project did show that significant gains in scholastic-ability test scores for preschool youngsters were attained when a special program of instruction was initiated. However, these gains were all but wiped out by the second grade with less than a two-point gain remaining.

As with physical, emotional, and social development, the intellectual variable contributes significantly to the complicated process of development of a student's self-concept.

We should understand that physical, social, emotional, and intellectual variables are linked together in the development of a person. The physical aspect is most readily identified, measured, and evaluated. Social, emotional, and intellectual factors are less identifiable but certainly as important.

The development of a student's self-concept tends to evolve through a process of differentiation and refinement; that is, new skills are developed and refined from gross or undisciplined ones. For example, in the area of motor development, the child learns to grasp with his whole hand, then slowly refines the use and function of the fingers in each hand. Later he develops sufficient control to write properly. Similarly, the child begins with less than perfect control over his emotions and slowly learns to differentiate feelings and emotions. He learns what anxiety, fear, aggression, and love are, and subsequently learns to deal with them effectively. Intellectually, the young child operates from a concrete world and only as he grows older can he move into a world of abstraction and theory.

Knowledge of the developmental processes should be of great importance to the teacher. If the teacher is to function effectively at a given level, she must know what to look for. She must be able to evaluate what she sees in terms of reasonable norms in order to develop an accurate perception and, consequently, a sound prescription for or approach to a child's problem. Perhaps a strictly academic treatment is needed, or it may be that an approach focuses on the child's social and emotional well-being. The teacher should view this introduction as a guide for better understanding of students, and the ways in which they develop and grow.

EXTERNAL-RANDOMIZED VARIABLES AND SELF-CONCEPT

Many changes continuously occur in the society at large bearing directly on the students' growth and development. All types of factors nurtured within the society are usually reflected outward to youngsters, impinging upon the developmental variables that we have reviewed. The effects of modern technology and communication, the pervasiveness of anomie and alienation, the increased use of drugs, contemporary changes in sexual folkways and mores, and the character of youth employment will be examined with regard to the ways in which these forces impinge on "normal" developmental patterns of students. What effects do these changes taking place in society have on the contemporary students' development of a sense of self?

Modern Technology and Communication

Often, changes that occur in the scientific realm have corresponding effects in the social sphere. The speedup of technology in the areas of communication and transportation have had an impact on youngsters. They see instantly, via television, what is happening in other parts of the world. They realize, too, the speed with which they can be "where the action is." Yet, for the most part, they are tied to a single setting within a relatively closed social system of family and friends. We are facing a problem of how to initiate a speedup in the student development of a realistic self corresponding to the accelerating pace of technology. If we can, by traveling in outer space, break the lockstep of "earth time" and move into a new dimension of measuring time relative to the speed of light, why can we not break the lockstep of our normal emotions and create a new dimension of emotions. The point here is not to justify travel in outer space, but instead to point to the dissonance between our technological and human achievements and to recognize the fact that these events make it more difficult for the student to focus with as much confidence as his predecessors upon the nature of "selfhood."

Increased Drug Usage

While intellectual, social, emotional, and physical growth are developmental factors extending over a relatively long period of time, the use of mind altering drugs is an attempt to produce a "short cut" to some new emotional state. Drug usage causes a dysfunction in one's normal emotional responses. This dysfunction can be viewed on a continuum from "occasional use" to "hard-core addict." Underscoring the nature of the problem, the United States Department of Justice (1971) recorded a 43 percent increase in drug addiction from 1960–1968, and a 1,860 percent increase in the number of drug arrests in this country. Numbers of addicts and arrests from the use of drugs grew from 44,906 to 64,011 and 37,752 to 134,006 respectively.

In a study of 150 college students of both sexes from three Eastern universities, Hertz (1970) found that 26 percent admitted to drug experimentation at some time. The illegality of drug usage may have posed a problem, leading the researcher to estimate that the use of marijuana, for example, may be as high as 50 percent and the use of amphetamines as high as 70 percent. Only 8 percent of the sample admitted to using LSD. In all cases, however, a new set of emotional norms is being established that is "out of step" with the previous emotional norms of students. Whether the use of drugs is caused by dissatisfaction with one's self-concept or through peer-group pressure, the problem of how to deal with this dysfunction remains. Schools have been attempting to remedy the problem with information campaigns about the harmful effects of drugs and the potential for addiction through repeated usage. Information, however, is not enough and sometimes even harmful; especially since much of the information regarding drugs has been cited as inaccurate. What is needed, in addition to accurate information, is a set of humane experiences that can help youngsters relate to one another more effectively without the use of drugs. There is a need for a well-developed affective curriculum, one in which feelings and emotions are explored and one in which we expose to youngsters the wide range of positive possibilities that can be found in the human experience.

Changes in Sexual Mores

Here again the new norms being established by youngsters appear to be quite different than those the older society had established. The mass media may be partly responsible for teasing youngsters unmercifully, presenting them with all of the superficialities and romanticizations of sex but without sufficient facts to deal with the realities. Wein (1970), after interviewing hundreds of teenagers across the country, concluded that "90 percent of American high school and junior high school students, no matter how sophisticated in other areas, are insecure and ill-informed about sex" (Wein, 1970, p. 12). While she found that there is more sexual activity among 17- and 18-year-olds today, she rarely found a liberated teenager who was free from guilt and fear about the act itself, and about reproduction and birth control. The *idea* of premarital intercourse seems quite acceptable among teenagers, yet there was very little evidence of a sexual revolution taking place. Wein further states that "A substantial change in sexual mores is slowly occurring, but revolutionaries generally have a certain amount of information at their command, and a degree of confidence. In regard to sex, these kids have neither. They are confused and cautious" (Wein, 1970, p. 12).

Other researchers have somewhat different findings to report. Broderick (1961, 1968) and his colleagues showed that the dating patterns of adolescent boys and girls have undergone marked changes in the past two decades. They studied fifth-, sixth-, and seventh-grade children, ages 10 to 13, since 1949 and found an increasing trend toward earlier dating. In 1949, for example, 15 percent of the boys and 20 percent of the girls dated. By 1958 the figures had risen to 45 percent for boys and 36 percent for girls. In 1968 their study showed 70 percent of boys and 53 percent of girls had dated.

The data showing the incidence of sexual intercourse has similarly undergone a noticeable change. In a recent study, Offer (1970) found that 10 percent of the boys had sexual intercourse at least once by the third year of high school. By the third year of college this figure had risen to 50 percent. For girls, however, the data is quite different. A survey, "Facts About Sexual Freedom," reported in *Education Digest* and conducted in 1968, revealed that 85 percent of 13- to 19-year-olds polled were virgins.

Sorensen (1973) conducted an extensive survey of adolescent sexual behavior, using 200 interviews and 411 confidential questionnaires from teenagers around the country, ranging in ages from 13 to 19 years of age. He found that 52 percent of teens have had sexual intercourse—59 percent of the boys and 45 percent of the girls. The most frequent age for first sexual intercourse varied, with 40 percent reporting that it took place in their sex partner's home, 20 percent reported that it took place in an automobile, 20 percent reported that it took place outdoors, with the remaining 20 percent occurred elsewhere.

Of the 48 percent of teenagers who had not experienced sexual intercourse, 22 percent of the boys and 25 percent of the girls were classified as "sexually inexperienced" because they had never more than kissed a member of the opposite sex. Seventeen percent were called "sexual beginners." This group reported all activities between plain kissing and intercourse, including petting to orgasm. The remaining 9 percent of the sample who had not had sexual intercourse were termed "unclassified virgins."

A rather dramatic change in sexual behavior seems to occur during the college years. Hertz (1970) selected a random sample of 150 undergraduate college students of both sexes from three Eastern universities. Sixty-one students were freshmen and sophomores and 89 were upperclassmen. Ninety-three students were male and 57 were female. Findings for the total sample indicated that 42 percent responded that the sexual act occurred "often," 19 percent "very often," 31 percent "a few times," and 8 percent "never." A separate analysis of the incidence of the sexual act for male and female was not given. However, it is interesting to note that only 8 percent of the sample "never" had sexual relations, while 92 percent of the students reported that they engaged in sexual relations, even if only "a few times."

These data indicate an increasing incidence of early dating and sexual relations among youngsters as they move through the adolescent years, and they reflect changing cultural norms with regard to sex.

Pervasiveness of Anomie and Alienation

Durkheim (1951) first introduced the term "anomie," which means normlessness, a moral vacuum, the suspension of rules—a state sometimes referred to as deregulation. Parsons (1951) referred to "anomie" as the "polar antithesis of full institutionalization . . . the absence of structured complementarity of the interaction process, or, what is the same thing, the complete breakdown of normative order" (Parsons, 1951, p. 30). Various works have been used to describe alienation. Seeman (1959) refers to it as powerlessness, meaninglessness, normlessness, isolation, and self-estrangement. In recent years we have seen an increase in alienation and anomie in our schools. On an institutional level, norms of behavior and dress, for example, have been suspended causing widespread anomie on the part of large segments of the school population. On a more personal level a greater number of students have either been caught up in the general wave of anomie or have imposed a form of self-isolation and estrangement on themselves. Regardless of whether the larger blame is with the individual or the institution, the problem is that we have growing alienation and anomie in our schools. Schools need to be aware of the nature of the phenomenon and initiate programs for groups and individuals that help either to reestablish old norms or to formulate new ones, the latter most likely being the case. Again, as with the drug problem, sound programs in affective education that can help alienated youngsters to achieve a feeling of cohesiveness and closeness with other human beings are desperately needed. Youngsters need guidance in handling natural emotions such as fear, aggression, anxiety, love, and belongingness. They need the experience of dealing successfully with these emotions. The student must discover the worthiness of his "self."

The Character of Youth Employment

Another variable that bears quite directly on the development of a student's self-concept is the success or failure in achieving work status in our society. Two factors mediate against youngsters with regard to employment. One is the extended period of adolescence in our society that holds youngsters back from achieving full status as adults. The second is the general economic situation. In 1969, for example, the United States Department of Labor, Bureau of Labor Statistics, reported that 11.4 percent of youth 16 to 24 years of age were unemployed and not enrolled in educational programs beyond high school. This was more than double the national average. Furthermore, in that same year, according to the United States Department of Commerce, Bureau of the Census, 16.8 percent of our youth dropped out of school before completing high school (1969).

Of the remaining youngsters, 41.1 percent were enrolled in school below the college level, and 16.6 percent were enrolled in college. Taken together, then, approximately 70 percent of our youth, ages 16 to 24, were either in school or unemployed. These data highlight the nature of the problem. If only 30 percent of our youth are able to test themselves in the reality of the "work world," then it is indeed true that the vast majority of youth are restrained from discovering and realizing their potential.

These data indicate that the need for improved career education programs in the schools, where youngsters receive realistic information and counsel about the opportunities and responsibilities they face on delayed entry into "the world of work." Modern students are forced through practical economic constraints to postpone their encounter with reality and the workaday world, delaying the much-needed reality testing so necessary for a realistic self-concept to emerge.

THE INTERFACE BETWEEN DEVELOPMENTAL AND EXTERNAL-RANDOMIZED VARIABLES

The developmental variables of physical, intellectual, social, and emotional growth as they interface with external-randomized factors such as drug usage, changing sexual mores, alienation and anomie, and youth employment were examined with some consideration given to the effects on a student's development of a sense of self. The developmental variables were described as developing over a period of time and were quite fundamental. The random variables tend to be everchanging, transitory, short range and less fundamental, but no less powerful. The student's selfhood develops through a combining and interconnecting of all of these factors. For example, a student lacking sufficient emotional stability (a developmental factor) may tend toward alienation or anomie (a random variable). The feeling of alienation or anomie may restrict his social development, perhaps impairing his normal needs (developmental). Youngsters may be faced with experiences in sexuality for which they are not emotionally prepared. Or, conversely, their emotional development may be such that it inhibits normal relationships between the sexes. Drugs do indeed alter a person's physical and emotional reactions and, conversely, his physical and emotional state may provide a predisposition toward taking drugs. One's physical, social, emotional, and intellectual development definitely affects the chances for success in the world of work and, certainly, success or failure at work can affect the development of self-concept.

What we have then are a myriad of variables interfacing with one another to produce "the student." What also becomes evident is that the interchange of forces among variables is unique for each student. We are led progressively, therefore, to the recognition of the importance of appreciating individual differences. Armed with a more sensitive and sophisticated understanding of how a student develops his or her self-concept, the teacher can go forward in helping particular students. This discussion, we expect, serves simply as a foothold, as the reader pursues his own inquiry into the enormous amount of lively material available on the American student today.

The teacher-centered selections that follow were taken from the practical, everyday concerns of three different teachers. They should serve the reader as vehicles for examination and discussion, bridging the often-considerable span between general theory and actual practice.

Theme 3 Today's Students

The student of today is a product of an environment vastly different from that of his predecessor. The bewildering effects of rapid and sometimes explosive change, one of the most significant characteristics of this decade, is central to the following selection. Physical changes in the young are relatively easy to discern. Students are measurably taller than their parents were. Track-and-field records continue to fall. Infinitely more difficult to ascertain, however, are the subtle differences in the affective domain: the value and attitudinal structure of today's youth.

Selection 3   INSTANT EDUCATION

Teacher: Alice Jenners
Age: 49
Experience: 26 years, secondary

Children today. There's no question at all that they are different. No question at all. Now I'm all for freedom. But freedom has become the password for everything. It's flaunted everywhere. Free schools, free thinking, open education. Certainly I'm for freedom . . . but for 12-year-olds? Come now. Let's be realistic.

Twelve-year-old children are just not mature enough to think freely for themselves, regardless of what the modern experts say. A youngster, 12-years-old, just doesn't have the depth of experience, of living to be able to render informed, intelligent opinions on everything from world trade to the liberalization of the state's divorce laws. They need to have lived a little longer, experienced a little bit more . . . and studied and thought a little harder and longer, too.

But today's parents and their children have no patience. It's "Give me everything right away. Right now, I've got to have it." No sense or comprehension that good things take time. The best fruit needs time to ripen. Good wine takes years. But this is the instant generation.

I guess I can understand them in some ways. You see, they've been raised on a diet of instant everything. Instant oatmeal. Instant news. Instant painkillers. Instant answers for everything. No wonder they've come to expect an instant education.

Last week I started a brand-new unit on social studies. Now before they have even finished reading the first chapter or had done any of the homework or any serious preparation, they were immediately

60

ready to have a debate. "Mrs. Jenners, can we have a debate? I'm pro, Mrs. Jenners, I'm pro. I'm against, Mrs. Jenners, I'm against." Now, my goodness, they were no more prepared to have a debate than I'm ready to dance on Broadway. But this is the way the children are these days. Unprepared, but oh, no shortage of confidence. But even then their confidence is paper thin. They're still fragile little children, and it's so very easy to poke holes in their pathetic little paper armor.

Probably the greatest shame of all with these young is their tremendous lack of respect for the great traditions and culture. They do not seem to understand the necessity for man to have rites and ceremonies . . . or that almost every situation today has had its historical antecedent. If the child of today does not get what he wants just when he wants it, then it is not "relevant," and you are accused of failing as a teacher!

Now with all of this reliance on instant gratification, it is no wonder that such a huge percentage of the young people today have turned toward drugs. If you're down, that's easily remedied, take an upper. If you're up, have no fear, take a downer. That's it. The age of easy remedies. But there's a terrible price to pay. You see, life was never designed to be easy, with easy and simple solutions for every problem. There is something to be said for the joy of the struggle, the battle to achieve.

What we need more than anything else in our schools today is a strong reemphasis on the old verities. More stress on the fundamentals, writing careful and complete sentences, expressing views after a thorough examination of the facts, not before. Above all, the taking of time to do things right. The best things this world has to offer were not built overnight. . . .

Suggestions for Further Study

1. Is Alice Jenners' position regarding "freedom for 12-year-olds," defensible from your point of view? What evidence from developmental psychology supports your position? What questions emanate from your reading of this case with regard to:

(a) Students and their needs for "instant gratification?"
(b) Values and value clarification processes of young people?
(c) The concept of "readiness" in relation to learning?
(d) The "real" changes in students today in comparison with other generations?
(e) The student drug culture?
(f) Alice Jenners' apparent approach to classroom teaching?

2. Invite a panel of three students from a nearby school to discuss the topic, "The difference between students today and students of yesteryear."

3. Interview, on tape, two experienced teachers with regard to their attitude toward students. What trends have been observed regarding the behavior of today's students in relation to the behavior of students two or three years ago? Ten years ago?

4. What additional issues are implicit in the case portrayed? Cite your position with regard to each issue identified. Support your view with appropriate research evidence.

Theme 4 Alienation

In many schools, students and teachers are pitted in an adversary relationship, each group attempting to outwit and outmaneuver the other. Such inauthentic relationships can lead to massive alienation. Alienation, defined as a state of being out of touch with others, is a term that has indeed been used to characterize much of our contemporary society. The central question generated by "Thirty Kids, Thirty Different Places," might well be, "What social and psychological conditions in and out of our schools seem to be significant factors in the growing feeling of alienation borne by both students and their teachers?" Eugene L., a teacher, shares his firsthand observations and concerns in the following soliloquy.

THIRTY KIDS,
THIRTY DIFFERENT PLACES

Teacher: Eugene Lowell
Age: 37
Experience: 15 years, junior and senior high school

Look at young Harrison out there. Long, messy hair. And that awful slouching in his seat. It's a wonder he doesn't fall on his ass. Uh-ah, watch it Gene old man . . . your prejudices are showing. After all, what's fundamentally wrong with long hair, or slouching?

You know, a teacher can look at a kid and, if for some reason, the teacher doesn't like the way he's dressed, or the way he speaks, or even the way he parts his hair . . . the teacher can communicate this in a glance. He doesn't need to say anything. Just a glance . . . and from that moment on the teacher and the student can be cut off from each other for the rest of the school year. That's how sensitive the teacher-student relationship is.

Yesterday I was talking with one of the so-called student radicals we have here. He said America was a sick country, and the remedy he offered was the burning down of Washington. At one level I got very upset, but at another level I calmed down. What came out was very calm. I said, "O.K. Rick, then what do you do after you do that?" Now when a kid says, "Let's burn down Washington," the general reaction of a teacher would normally tend to be so strong and so defensive that the communication between the student and the teacher would never get to the next step. Yet, it is at this next step that communication can really begin.

If a kid in my math class says that my course is totally irrelevant to his life, I accept that. I never defend what I'm doing and I never

64

defend the system either. In fact, sometimes, when it's warranted, I go along and agree that change is necessary. Sometimes, I'll just probe for more information on the student's attitude. You see, as soon as you put yourself in the position where you are against the position the student has taken, you create an atmosphere where both persons became rigid . . . and this leads to a stifling of further discussion. It cuts off communication just at the point where communication is most necessary.

You really can't take students for granted. See, when you're up there in front of the classroom, each kid out there is in a different place. Thirty kids, thirty different places. I once had a bright and charming girl in my math class who won the math medal for outstanding performance. Then in the very next year she had to drop out of school because she had gotten pregnant. This year, I have a boy who comes to class every day but never participates in anything. He does none of the work. I tried everything, but nothing I did could get him involved. Just last week I found out that his old man is an alcoholic who doesn't live at home. The old man corners the kid every morning outside the house and cons the boy out of his lunch money. No wonder the boy hasn't been able to concentrate . . . he's been thinking about his morning meetings with his father rather than my formulas and board work. All kinds of things are going on in kids' minds while they're facing you. All kinds of things.

And even the kids don't seem to be listening to each other. They've got their own factions. The academic types versus the jocks. The conservatives versus the radicals. Soccer players versus football players. Cheerleaders versus other girls. All closed groups. Something is very wrong here. Yes, both teachers and students need help in hearing each other.

Suggestions for Further Study

1. What would be the probable consequence of a teacher's emotional and negative response if a student were to suggest something transparently outrageous, as in this case "Let's burn down Washington!"? Would you have re-

sponded differently than Eugene Lowell? Discuss alternate approaches and their probable consequences to student-teacher relationships.

2. Do your personal observations tend to confirm Eugene Lowell's contention that there is a growing degree of alienation in the schools? If so, what social and psychological factors do you believe may be contributing to this trend? Document evidence to buttress your view, when possible. What can you, personally, contribute toward lessening the extent of alienating conditions in both the schools and the larger society as well?

3. Observe a class in a nearby school or university and search for clues as to whether genuine listening seems to be taking place:
   (a) Teacher to student.
   (b) Student to teacher.
   (c) Student to student.
   (d) Groups of students to other groups of students.
   Describe the *quality* of listening that you have observed. What specifically can you recommend to improve the character of the communication processes that you have observed? What will you do to improve communication conditions between you and your students? What is your view toward the value of sensitivity training, encounter and T-groups in helping improve various interpersonal relationships? What research evidence can you muster to support your position?

4. Numerous studies and articles have been written regarding loneliness and alienation in contemporary America. What aspects from the literature can you identify that specifically relates to issues implicit to this selection? Show concisely the application of the literature to the selection.

5. Compose a panel of several students and teachers to discuss the quality of interpersonal relationships between students and teachers in their particular schools.

6. Try to learn more about the value of listening to other persons. Make it a point to listen to someone more deeply than

ever before. Have someone observe and comment on your capacity for listening and caring.

7. Select a particular student that interests you. Review carefully his or her cumulative folder in the school file, if possible. Conduct a thorough case study of this student, using an appropriate case study guide. (You might want to use the case study checklist found on pp. 24–27.)

Theme 5 Disadvantaged Youth

Recently, much attention, though often insufficient *action*, has been focused upon the inferior conditions of learning of minority groups in America. Puerto Ricans, American Indians, Chicanos, blacks and the poor, are among those often characterized as educationally disadvantaged. The schools represent the primary arena where the confrontation is taking place between America's "haves" and "have nots." The lasting effects on the psyche of America's young is something with which we have yet to deal. One teacher's trying effort to alter a prevalent attitude of white middle-class apathy in his school district is portrayed in the ensuing capsule.

Selection 5   WHY I TRY TO TEACH WHITE KIDS
IN MY FRENCH CLASSES WHATEVER
I CAN REGARDING THE DISADVANTAGED

Teacher: William Talcott
Age: 29
Experience: 7 years, secondary

Here is the point: they build a white school, so to speak, in a black neighborhood and they don't invite the community members to work with them in the planning of it. No wonder the blacks want to tear the place down. And the white kids here don't really understand. That's why I try to teach the white kids in my French class whatever I can regarding the disadvantaged. After all, white kids and their parents, their family and their way of living seem to be the dominant destructive forces in the lives of the black people anyway. I teach my French class about black peoples, black history, and black contributions. After all, it's not being taught in the social studies classes here.

Other controversial issues such as Vietnam, are also verboten topics in social studies, except perhaps where Vietnam is located geographically. The negative, embarrassing issues are sidestepped. The same with black history. Look for yourself at our social studies textbooks and you will see how black history is just glossed over. Oh, you'll find black people represented by George Washington Carver and Booker T. Washington. And in some of the more-recent texts you might find some reference to King's march on Washington. But there's no mention of the real, real blacks. No mention of Malcolm X, Eldridge Cleaver, Bobby Seale, George Jackson, Attica, the Black Panthers. It's as if they never existed.

And my fellow faculty members are such hypocrites too. The principal once invited me to share some of the things I learned at a summer institute on black studies at one of our faculty meetings. But, I found out the hard way that the man was not really interested in spreading the institute's ideas at all. He was just feigning an interest in blacks as a showcase for his faculty meeting. That's all. He passed over my ideas as if they were small jokes. I vow, I'll never forget that.

When I first came back from that summer institute, I tried to tell people about my experiences—where they could find materials, how they could more effectively teach the disadvantaged. But all I seemed to get from most of my teaching colleagues was a nice smile and a little lip service at best. What seemed to happen was that my white colleagues did not, in any way, really want to relinquish any part of what they had. What they want, they say, is for the black kids to come at least halfway. "If the blacks want help, then they've got to start to pull themselves up!"

You would think educated people—professional teachers—would realize that these kids do not have the tools to come halfway. And then why should they come halfway to the white way of living? Maybe, they despise our way of living. Maybe there is something to be despised about it. Blacks often think, "Whitey, my way of living hasn't been too good these past 350 years." Many black kids have developed a terrific hatred for the white power structure and it's become more and more internal than on the surface. But for some reason they have come to trust me. It took me more than three long years of hard work to establish this trust, but it's there now. I'm sure of it.

However, if I simply settled for working on improving black-white relations only in this school, then I would not have had any success to speak of. See, a white teacher has to go out of his way to prove his worthiness to a black kid. A lot of white liberals resent this. They say, "I know that I'm worthy, why do I have to prove anything?" They should remember that over the years, over 350 years, a great deal of mistrust has been built up. Anyway, it's quite difficult, but you know, there are two black teachers in our school, and if a black student has a problem, he will definitely contact me before he will go to them. For the first couple of years, I was constantly being tested, but not anymore. If they thought for one minute that I was insincere, then they would turn me completely off. That's the way it is with young blacks. You can't fake them. They can tell if you feel what you profess, inside, at the gut level.

Unfortunately, I'm making very little forward progress with my colleagues in this school. Whereas a year ago, the teachers would listen to my suggestions and say "no" outright, now they say "yes" but still don't do anything. That kind of resistance is very insidious. Some of the new, young teachers try but, more often than not, they get themselves in a whole lot of trouble with both the whites and blacks as a result of their inexperience.

There are just a handful of blacks in this school and they need help desperately. But very few teachers really want to do anything, except talk. They talk while I act. Yes sir. I try, at every opportunity, to teach the white kids in my French classes all I can about the disadvantaged. . . .

Suggestions for Further Study

1. William Talcott has expressed his stringent and very direct opinions. With which particular aspects of his position do you agree? Disagree? Discuss the rationale for *your* opinion. What logical support can you muster for your position?
2. Identify some of the more-significant issues in this case that clearly relate to the psychological development of various students. Formulate these issues into concise questions. Refer to the "answer finding" section on p. 169 and proceed, step by step, to develop soundly conceived positions with regard to questions that you raised.
3. To what extent is black history accurately represented in the textbooks of a nearby school system? Cite sources of evidence and state your specific findings. Did you rely on primary or secondary sources of evidence to determine the accuracy of the history? Discuss.
4. It has been said that the adolescent years are certainly the most critical in developing a realistic self-concept. To what

extent does this case relate to self-concept theory? What effects on student self-concept is William Talcott likely to have?

5. What are some of the special problems involved that are peculiar to teaching disadvantaged as opposed to more-advantaged youths? In what way would you suppose your teaching strategies would have to differ, if at all? What do you plan to do personally, if anything, in terms of preparing to help the educationally disadvantaged?

6. Describe "the disadvantaged" in a nearby school system. Interview one of the teachers of the disadvantaged in that school and compare that teacher's views with the ideas of William Talcott.

7. Develop a panel composed of a number of secondary school students. Include a mixture of "advantaged" and "disadvantaged" students. Read aloud the case of William Talcott and have an open panel discussion in which the students react to the case.

Annotated Bibliography

Ausubel, David P. *Psychology: A Cognitive View.* New York: Holt, Rinehart and Winston, Inc., 1968. One of the most prolific writers in the field gives an excellent presentation of the role of cognition in human learning.

Bartlett, F. C. *Thinking: An Experimental and Social Study.* London: G. Allen, 1958. A penetrating study of thinking and how one thinks when presented with complex structures.

Erikson, Erik. *Childhood and Society.* New York: W. W. Norton, 1950. Presents one of the few comprehensive theories of ego development from birth through retirement years. Although the author maintains a deterministic posture, the theory is useful in providing guideposts to social and emotional development.

Gessell, Arnold, et al. *The First Five Years of Life: A Guide to the Study of the Preschool Child.* New York: Harper, 1940.

One of several books on the developmental processes of the child. While much of the material is in narrative form and some of it tends to be subjective, it is an extremely useful text.

Havighurst, Robert. *Developmental Tasks and Education.* New York: Longmans, 1951. Discusses the author's concept of the developmental task and presents a sequence of such tasks to be mastered by the child as he develops.

Lindgren, Henry C. and Fredrica Lindgren. *Current Readings in Educational Psychology.* New York: John Wiley and Sons, 1971. An up-to-date and well-developed set of readings that provide an excellent overview of the field of educational psychology.

Piaget, Jean. *Language and Thought of the Child.* London: Routledge and Kegan Paul, 1926. A classic treatise on the cognitive development of children. The author utilizes the interview technique and postulates theoretical propositions from the empirical data gathered in the study.

Skinner, B. F. *Walden Two.* New York: Macmillan, 1948. Describes a society in which the behaviorist tenets of conditioning applied to learning are utilized.

Terman, L. M., et al. *Mental and Physical Traits of a Thousand Gifted Children.* Stanford, California: Stanford University Press, 1925. A classic study of gifted children. Many of the findings of the authors tend to modify the stereotype view of gifted youngsters as being odd or primarily introverted.

Torrance, E. Paul. *Rewarding Creative Behavior: Experiments in Classroom Activity.* Englewood Cliffs, N.J.: Prentice-Hall, 1965. The author discusses findings from his research on the creativity of school-age children. He has categorized creative acts according to recurring patterns that were discovered during his study.

Section III THE PROCESS

Here we examine both learning and teaching processes. One should recognize that the learning act can occur without an act of teaching preceding it. That is, learning on the part of persons is rarely ever completely dependent on teaching. People often learn without teachers. But the converse is not true. Teaching is very much dependent on learning. In fact, it is reasonable to state that teaching is virtually impossible without some kind of learning ensuing, at least, effective teaching!

We will study learning and learning theory at the outset, then we will review some theory related to teaching processes. In the third and final portion of this introduction, we consider, in sequence (1) the interplay between teaching and learning in both formal and informal classroom situations with some critical review of various teaching modalities and techniques employed in the classroom and (2) the means of appraising outcomes of the learning-teaching processes. These means include various methods of appraising students, such as aptitude, personality and achievement testing, and consideration of the effects of marks and marking systems.

LEARNING

Learning, What Is It?

A simplified version of a learning event can be illustrated as follows:

75

"What is your name?" the child asks.
"My name is Mr. Truth," the man replies.
Two days later, the child upon meeting the same man
says, "Hello, Mr. Truth."

It becomes obvious that the child has indeed learned the
man's name. Learning has taken place.

Professor Robert Gagné, who has written widely regarding
learning theory, affords us a straightforward definition of learning, "Learning is a change in human disposition or capability
which can be retained and which is not simply ascribable to
the process of growth" (Gagné, 1970, p. 3). The change in
human disposition might have to do with a person's attitude or
values. Capability refers to a type of performance, as in the
preceding instance, where the child was able to perform, that
is, to state Mr. Truth's name upon meeting him and, of course,
that particular act was certainly not simply ascribable to the
natural processes of genetic or physical growth.

Theoretical Considerations Regarding Learning

Theories of learning are attempts to explain how learning
takes place. When learning takes place the phenomenon can
be viewed and explained from various perspectives. One
theory would undoubtedly emphasize one aspect of the process to a greater extent than another, yet the explanation of
why learning occurred can be accommodated by various other
theories as well. No one theory is gospel. They are, after all,
theories rather than laws.

What seems necessary for the practicing teacher is an answer to the questions Which ones of the various efforts that he
makes effectively produce learning? *How* do these efforts produce learning? Any method employed by the teacher that continuously failed to produce student learning should, it would
seem, be discarded regardless of how sound the theoretical rationale appeared on paper.

Probably for this reason many teachers strenuously avoid
serious discussions of learning theory. Yet some unifying explanation of the learning phenomena can serve the teacher

well. Instead of a potpourri of random techniques, a theoretical position (no matter how tentative) can afford the teacher a comprehensive point of view and can provide the teacher with a basis for developing unique approaches to the myriad situations that he encounters in the classroom.

Professor Ernest R. Hilgard (1956) concluded, in his important and comprehensive work, *Theories of Learning*, that "there are no laws of learning that can be taught with confidence" (Hilgard 1956, p. 326). Most learning psychologists would like to offer an absolute position but few would dare, and those that do seem destined to miss the mark.

Types of Learning Theories:
Connectionism and Perceptionism

Learning psychologists have organized their discussions regarding various learning theories in a number of ways. Clayton (1965) places various theories into three broad categories that he labels (1) the specificists, composed largely of those relying on the stimulus-response principle, (2) the field theorists, who concentrated largely on the domain of perception, cognition, and psychomotor activity and, finally (3) the personality and motivation theorists who dwelt on the nature of a person's "being."

Bugelski (1971), in his highly regarded educational psychology text, features only two learning theorists—Pavlov and Thorndike—instead of the whole range of theoretical positions. He observed little difference in the two, summarizing ". . . both theorists can be described as objectivistic and as believing in learning as the necessary result of environmental manipulation. Pavlov manipulated stimuli; Thorndike manipulated rewards" (Bugelski, 1971, p. 68). A broader, more encompassing treatment of learning theorists is employed by Kuethe (1968). He categorizes theories in terms of their being either connectionist or nonconnectionist. We chose here to classify the various theories as either connectionist (Kuethe's term) or perceptionist, which we will describe later. First let us consider connectionistic learning theory.

Pavlov and Thorndike, in addition to numerous others, are

both viewed as connectionist. Aristotle, and his treatment of the nature of memory and its relationship to the concepts of similarity, contrast, and contiguity of ideas, is identified as antecedent to modern-day connectionism. Thomas Hobbes (1588–1679), usually identified with the English school of associationism, and John Locke (1634–1704), who spoke of "connections" or combinations of ideas in his "Essay on Human Understanding" (1690), are credited as pioneer thinkers in early connectionistic thought. David Hume's (1711–1776) very important contribution to connectionist thought was his observation that when ideas come together or "connect" they should be regarded as a tendency rather than an absolutely predictable event. Kuethe elaborated on this point.

> The influence of this notion is seen today in the fact that association data are treated statistically rather than by analysis based on all or nothing models. As a result of empirical study, it becomes possible to state the probability that a particular association will occur in a given population or for a particular individual. There is, however, no guarantee that a certain association will occur every time. The notion that associations may result from elements that are linked through other elements was Hume's anticipation of what is now referred to as *mediated association.* For example, the word "red" lead to "cow" through the mediation of the concept "barn." Such chains may be quite long and complex, branching in many directions and they contribute to the richness and diversity of human thought.
>
> (Kuethe, 1968, pp. 20–21)

The philosophical ideas of David Hartey (1707–1757), James Mill (1773–1836), John Stuart Mill (1806–1873), and Johann Friedrich Herbert (1776–1841), must also be regarded as fundamental to the connectionist school.

Connectionist theory, as more recently developed by E. L. Thorndike, stated that learning results from the strengthening of connections or bonds in the brain. The more that a person learns, the more useful connections he will have and hence, the more educated he will be. In 1898 Thorndike published his theory of learning based largely on a number of animal experiments and using a trial-and-error model. The Russian, Pavlov, in his well-known experiment (Pavlov's dog) in which he established a "connection" *without* relying on trial and error wherein he paired simultaneously, both a bell and a dog's salivation, illustrates still another dimension of connectionism.

Psychologist Clark Hull subsequently developed a complex reinforcement theory, and, most recently, B. F. Skinner's reinforcement theories have received much attention. Skinner's theory utilizes an operant-conditioning principle, emphasizing carefully dispersed positive reinforcements (M & Ms, praise words) and negative reinforcements (teacher scolding) to manage behavior.

The student of learning theory will find a substantial body of useful information in Skinner's writings. The other school of thought that we categorized as "the perceptionist group" also will afford the teacher additional and useful theoretical propositions.

Perceptionist Learning Theories

The perceptionists give greater emphasis to the internal, less-visible aspects of learning, the state of mind of the learner, and the unique *perceptions* of a person, rather than the clearly more-observable behaviors or outcomes of the learning process that pertain to connectionism.

Max Wertheimer, Kurt Koffka, and Wolfgang Kohler are identified as *Gestalt* psychologists and fit into the perceptionist category. The underlying principle of the Gestaltist is "The whole is greater than the sum of its parts." This concept can be readily understood by undertaking an experiment. Have several rather well-known male members of a group step outside of the room. Arrange for one of these persons to expose only his hand at the doorway. Ask the persons who have remained in the room to identify whose hand appeared. It is likely that very few, if any, will be able to match with any degree of certainty the correct hand with the correct person. This is because when most of us relate to a *person* we relate to a "wholeness" rather than to a part of a person. A person, according to the Gestaltist, is very much more than simply a sum of his parts, although mathematically this may not be true. So it is, say the Gestaltists, with many other perceived phenomena. Again, the whole is greater than the mathematical sum of its parts.

Kurt Lewin's (1948) field theory concerned itself strongly with perception, cognition, and action and has a very clear application to the work of the teacher. Lewin, just as much as the earlier Gestaltists, chose to pay heed to internal arrangements—the cognitive field of the individual. He concurred that behavior was a function of perception, but he viewed the cognitive field as partly dependent on field forces in a world outside the learner. The life space of each of us is the way we have come to perceive and interact with the external world. The psychological life space that each of us carries is quite unique. This psychological world is composed of our changing attitudes, values, fantasies, aspirations, and goals at any given moment. A version of the life space of a college student can be illustrated as on page 81.

Heavy and weak, positive and negative vectors of force between various areas within the life space can be drawn indicating the character of various intrapsychic relationships. The distance between and location of the various elements in the life space of a given individual has meaning also. The life space of any individual, it should be recognized, is undergoing continuous change and, therefore, the illustration represents a single point in time, rather than a fixed or durable picture. The life space picture of one month to the next is likely to be quite different.

The late Fritz Perls (1969), known as the founder of Gestalt therapy, developed an intriguing approach to individual and group psychotherapy focusing on the intrapsychic relationships of a person (Lewin's life space), with emphasis on personal awareness on the "now" as opposed to the past or future.

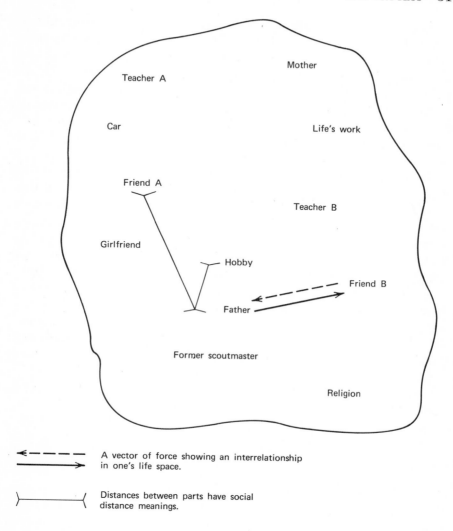

A vector of force showing an interrelationship in one's life space.

Distances between parts have social distance meanings.

The phenomenologists, exemplified by Combs and Snygg (1959), also based their position on the assumption "as we perceive, we behave." The phenomenological position is clearly allied with the Gestaltist, the field theorist, and others designated as perceptionists.

A review of learning theory without taking John Dewey into account cannot be justified. His influence on the development of modern learning theory is indisputable, yet a comprehensive analysis of his position regarding learning theory has never really been achieved. Dewey is customarily viewed as an educational philosopher rather than a psychologist. However, in terms of learning theory he seems clearly positioned in the perceptionist camp. For Dewey, stimulus and response were viewed as intimately related, but mediated, experiences. He was opposed to the connectionist position that specifically separates stimulus from response.

Perhaps Edward C. Tolman, more than any other psychologist, has bridged the gap between the connectionists and the perceptionists. Tolman, a behaviorist in method, subscribed to many of the theoretical positions of Lewin and other perceptionists. For example, Tolman presented experimental evidence demonstrating that rats seek out appropriate stimuli and were not merely "pawns" responding to given stimuli. Rats manifest a capacity to choose, according to Tolman's scientific observations. He has been termed by some as a "field behaviorist," which may at first seem to be a contradiction in terms. But he utilized Gestaltist ideology and Lewin's field-theory and life-space concepts yet, true to the behaviorist tradition, he attempted to validate what he termed "cognitive maps" with rigorous data obtained from *objective*, nonverbal, controlled animal behavior.

The fundamental differences between the stimulus-response theorists (described here as connectionists) and the stimulus-*perception*-response theorists (that we have classified as perceptionists) have been examined. The views of Lewin, Tolman, Skinner, and Thorndike, of both connectionists and perceptionists each have value with each affording the teacher another useful way of understanding learning.

TEACHING

Teaching, What Is It?

Teaching has not been adequately defined. Gilbert Highet, in *The Art of Teaching* (1950), holds no brief with those who define teaching as a science instead of as an art. Highet compares a teacher to an artist as he paints or to the composer as he creates a symphony. Probably, for most, it seems acceptable to define teaching as placed somewhere between an art and a science. A review of some of the research regarding the teaching process is an effort to view some scientific aspects of the process.

Teaching as a Science

N. L. Gage, who developed the well-regarded *Handbook on Teaching*, cautions us not to belittle efforts to scientifically examine teaching. Let us examine some of the more-promising research forays into teaching that have been undertaken.

B. J. Biddle (1964), on reviewing much of the research regarding teaching effectiveness, sadly concluded that after 40 years of research we still do not know how to define, prepare for, or measure teacher competence. Efforts to correlate such variables as teachers' attitudes, values, background, and personality factors with teaching effectiveness have not panned out. Then what does make one teacher more effective than another?

The work of Ned Flanders (1960) has made some inroad into this question. Flanders developed a unique procedure for analyzing the character of interaction between teacher and students in the classroom. One dimension of his system included an analysis of the quality of "teacher talk." Flanders found that teachers who most often offered praise and an acceptance of student feelings and ideas produced a higher degree of student achievement (with regard to the particular subject matter of the class) than did the teachers who did not act similarly.

Similarly, Carl Rogers (1969), a noted psychotherapist and distinguished educator, has also established, through a number of research studies, that responding to students and clients in a positive way (i.e., holding an unconditional positive regard for the personhood of students and listening empathically to their ideas and feelings) produced deeper and more-lasting learning.

Some very interesting research on students' views of the quality of instruction has been produced recently. College students in particular, largely as a consequence of the intense student unrest manifested on American campuses, have participated in evaluating the quality of faculty instruction. Costin, Grennough, and Menges (1971) reviewed and summarized the findings of over 100 articles and studies regarding students' evaluation of their instructors. Certainly the ultimate consumers of instruction (i.e., students) have much to offer in defining and assessing the quality of teaching to which they have been and are subjected.

Costin and his colleagues extricated some interesting and pertinent data. Student opinions, as far as what constitutes a good teacher, often included such teacher attributes as (1) preparedness, (2) clarity of presentation, and (3) ability to stimulate intellectual curiosity. (Costin, et al., 1971, p. 516). Experienced professors usually received higher ratings than did their less-experienced colleagues. It was noted that teaching effectiveness and research activity by professors were not necessarily correlative. Correlating *positively* with teaching effectiveness were students' ratings of teachers' agreeableness, emotional stability, and enthusiasm.

The work of B. S. Bloom should be noted. Bloom (1956) and several associates developed a systematic classification scheme for various educational objectives. Delineation of these objectives has furnished assistance to researchers and thinkers who are attempting to carefully assess and uniformly describe teaching outcomes. Bloom's classification scheme (taxonomy) describes with care and precision the various kinds of behaviors that can be expected from students. This taxonomy is divided into three domains: cognitive, affective, and psychomotor. The cognitive focuses on objectives having to do with thinking, knowing, and problem solving; the affective concentrates largely on emotional conditions such as values, attitudes, and interests; the psychomotor domain (yet to be completed) deals with performance activities utilizing manual and motor skills (such as work). All learning outcomes can, using various taxonomies, be uniformly delineated in terms of specific behaviors and actions (Bloom, 1956, pp. 62–67). For example, evidence of knowledge (one of the primary behavioral objectives expected by most teachers) is classified as follows: 1.00—knowledge, with subgroups 1.10—knowledge of specifics, 1.11—knowledge of terminology, 1.12—knowledge of specific facts, and so forth (Bloom, 1956, pp. 62–67). Each of these objectives is fully described in terms of pupil performance. If one of the expected outcomes of a social studies lesson, for example, is to be familiar with the term "legislature," it would fit into category 1.11—knowledge of terminology. Theoretically, all objectives in education can be appropriately classified, although, of course, the classification of some objectives are inherently more difficult than others. In any event, the scheme offers researchers a standardized approach to the already sufficiently complex task of studying the effects of teaching on student behaviors.

Among the most-promising research areas regarding teaching effectiveness is a teacher quality that has been described as the cognitive flexibility-rigidity construct. This construct refers to "the teacher's ability to think on his feet, to adapt teaching objectives, content and method as he teaches" (Mosher, 1967, p. 125) in accordance with the reaction, learning difficulties, and verbal "feedback" from the students. "Cognitive flexibility, as a psychological concept, refers to the teachers' capacity for open-mindedness, adaptability, and resistance to premature perceptual closure" (Mosher, 1967, p. 125). Rokeach (1954) and his studies of "openness" and "closedness" of belief systems precede the development of the cognitive flexibility-rigidity construct. Rokeach's development of a scale measuring dogmatism was, in essence, an early effort attempting to determine whether a person is relatively open- or closed-minded, a factor certainly related to cognitive flexibility-rigidity.

The hypothesis that cognitive flexibility produces effective teaching has been supported by some noteworthy studies (Emlaw, Mosher, Sprinthall, and Whitely, 1963). Briefly, in one of these studies, 28 subjects, randomly selected from the population of student teachers in the Harvard-Newton Summer Program in 1964, were administered two projective psychological tests (the Rorschach and the Visual Impressions

Test) before beginning their practice teaching. While student teaching, the cognitive style of the subjects with regard to their flexible and rigid teaching behaviors were evaluated by supervisors with a teacher-rating scale. The ratings were based on a complete class period of the subject's teaching as well as various supervisory and planning conferences. The subjects were, in this manner, judged as being among (1) the most flexible, (2) the moderate, or (3) the most rigid in their cognitive approach to teaching. Follow-up (i.e., verifying the future success of the subject in terms of succeeding in the teaching program in a regular teaching position) yielded data that clearly indicated that the predicting methods were highly accurate. Two subsequent studies, replicating the preceding one, produced almost identical results; teacher cognitive flexibility does appear as an important ingredient in effective teaching.

Can cognitive flexibility be learned? "The weight of theoretical evidence tends to suggest that a disposition to flexibility-rigidity is another of the 'by age five' phenomena. It is obviously difficult, if not impossible for most persons to develop this trait in later years" (Mosher, 1967, p. 130). However, it is likely that even limited cognitive-flexibility attributes instilled at an early age, can be enlarged upon and refined through improved teacher training.

Although several studies support the virtue of cognitive flexibility toward affective teaching (Yee, 1967; Coogan, 1958; McGee, 1955; Ryans, 1960), there seems to be some semantic looseness. For example, Gage (1970), in noting the similarity in findings of a number of studies on teaching effectiveness, stated that "Although any single term is inadequate (to describe the findings), it seems safe to use the term 'warmth.' Teacher warmth, seems, on the basis of abundant and varied research evidence, to be quite defensible as a desirable characteristic of teachers" (Gage, 1970, p. 124). Warmth is a pervasive, perhaps too-general term. "Nonpossessive warmth" as coined by Rogers, probably more clearly describes this desirable teacher attribute. Nonpossessive warmth suggests a warmth that does not suffocate.

The ability to induce discovery (Flanders, 1960) and a quality described as a cognitive organization facility (Ausubel, 1963) have also proved to be important teacher attributes. The first—inducing "learning by discovery"—is self-explanatory. Cognitive organization, perhaps more vague, suggests the ability for a teacher to structure the learning of subject matter into orderly, step by step, progressive procedures. A good example is found in the systematic approach that gradually introduces more and more difficult ideas and concepts as found in soundly developed programmed learning devices or "teaching machines."

Rogers (1969) presents a useful model for teaching that incorporates much of the results of the research that we cited. The teacher, as Rogers describes him, is a "facilitator of learning," one who helps develop a warm learning environment giving the student an opportunity to learn in his own way and essentially on his own terms. Rogers emphasizes the nurturance of a student's *intrinsic* capabilities to learn. He suggests that teachers help students generate the ability to be "self-starters" in learning, rather than pawns dependent largely on externally imposed motivational factors.

Rogers' principles of client-centered therapy readily encompass an approach toward student-centered teaching. The teacher, in attempting to create an effective learning environment, must see to it that he provides the prospective learner with the identical conditions that the therapists offer in client-centered therapy. These conditions are (1) unconditional positive regard toward the client (student), (2) empathic understanding of the student, and (3) congruence on the part of the therapist or teacher (Rogers, 1969, p. 116). Each of these is described briefly:

Unconditional positive regard means, essentially, that the client-learner must be *accepted* on his own terms. For example, if the student differs from the teacher (or therapist), that is, has a vastly different value system such as believing in legalizing abortions while the teacher holds the opposite view, the teacher must take no offense. In fact, if the teacher is to truly manifest unconditional positive regard, he must fully accept the *affective* position of the student. This, of course, is a quite unnatural condition. The natural response of most mortals would be to take exception to the affective position of a person with an emotional view strongly opposed to one's own. Holding unconditional positive regard for some students is a difficult, yet necessary, requisite in this approach.

The second factor, empathic caring for the student and his world, is an unnatural quality for most teachers. Sympathy, feeling sorry *for,* is a more-common trait. "Poor child, comes from such a wretched home" denotes sympathy. Empathy, on the other hand, suggests feeling *with* rather than a feeling *for* or *toward* something. Holding sympathy for someone tends to place the teacher in a somewhat "holier than thou" mindset. This is what Martin Buber (1965), a renowned existentialist philosopher, described as an "I-It" relationship, making persons objects rather than people. Buber's "I-Thou" relationship illustrates a teacher identifying a student as a person rather than an object. With empathy the teacher listens *deeply* to the student. He hears the student not just with his ears but with his whole being, attempting to *feel* as if he were the student, as the student shares.

Finally, the teacher, using this approach, must attempt to be personally congruent, that is, authentic. Congruence, Rogers explains, means "To be genuine or honest or real, means to be this way about *oneself.* I cannot be real about another," he says, "because I do not know what is real for him. I can only tell, if I wish to be truly honest, what is going on in me. Let me take an example. Early in this chapter I reported Miss Shiel's feelings about the 'mess' created by the art work. Essentially she said, 'I find it maddening to live with the mess! I'm neat and orderly and it is driving me to distraction'. But suppose her feelings had come out somewhat differently, in the disguised way which is much more common in classrooms at all levels. She might have said, '*You* are the messiest children I've ever seen! *You* don't care about tidiness or cleanliness. *You* are just terrible!' This is most definitely not an example of genuiness or realness . . ." (Rogers, 1969, p. 113).

In the first illustration, Miss Shiel, as Rogers described her, was sharing her perception of what was going on *inside* her.

She looked toward and found part of her, "*I'm* neat and orderly and its driving *me*. . . ." She was searching and finding inside herself. In the second instance, she did not search and of course, did not find anything within herself to share, "*You* are the messiest . . . *You* don't care . . . *You* are just . . . etc." "You," of course, refers to the students. So, in the second situation that Rogers described, the teacher did not exhibit congruence.

When a teacher is able to successfully hold the qualities of unconditional positive regard, empathic understanding and *self*-congruence, it can be expected that the student will be inclined to feel freer and comfortable enough to test his own learning capacities. Student-centered teaching, although on the surface appearing to radically differ from behavioristic tenets, such as found in programmed instruction, is not really incompatible with other teaching approaches, as we shall see later on.

Gage (1968) has suggested that teaching may be too complex to study as a holistic entity. The teaching process can be viewed as multifaceted. Further headway might be made if one studies particular segments of teaching. This kind of teaching is called microteaching and Gage has suggested that we judge the outcomes of such teaching with appropriate "microcriteria."

> If the global criterion approach has proven to be sterile, what (is) the alternative? The answer (is) to take the same path that more mature sciences had already followed: If variables at one level of phenomena do not exhibit lawfulness, break them down. Chemistry, physics and biology had, in a sense, made progress through making finer and finer analysis of the phenomena and events they dealt with. Perhaps research on teaching would reach firm ground if it followed the same route.
>
> (Gage, 1968, p. 602)

He suggests evaluating microteaching with more-appropriate criteria:

Rather than seek criteria for the over all effectiveness of teachers in the many varied facets of their roles, we may have better success with criteria of effectiveness in small, specifically designed aspects of the role . . . a sufficient number of laws applying to relatively pure aspects of the teacher's role, if such laws could be developed, might eventually be combined . . . to account for the actual behavior and effectiveness of teachers with pupils under genuine classroom conditions.

(Gage, 1963, p. 120)

Progress in emphasizing "microcriteria" in conjunction with "microteaching" has been reported at the Stanford Center for Research and Development in Teaching. In microteaching, the process of teaching is divided into its component instructional parts, such as the ability to establish rapport with students and effective use of questions. A short lesson employing only *one* of these measurable skills is taught and its effectiveness is rated using one or more of the microcriteria, for example, did students respond trustfully (indicating rapport). Research on teaching effectiveness is greatly simplified. The inherent difficulty, however, becomes apparent when one raises the Gestaltist question, "Isn't teaching more than the mere sum of its parts?"

Teaching, in the final analysis, may be as Highet (1950) suggested, totally an art. The practice of teaching is, most certainly, largely an art form. But teachers owe it to themselves and, more importantly, to their students to incorporate the most-significant findings from research and science into their prevailing practices.

OTHER FACTORS: TRANSFER AND MOTIVATION

Transfer of Learning

It was, at one time, widely held that the vigorous study of Greek, Latin, algebra, and geometry were vital not simply for their own uses but also because the mental discipline required for their mastery would transfer over into many other walks of life. It was presumed that such exercise "trained the muscles of the mind." Such has been shown not to be the case, although many teachers and other educators and lay persons somehow still cling to such a logical seeming myth. The facts have proved quite contrary, however. This "mental discipline" doctrine was first challenged by psychologist William James. James found no improvement in his own ability to memorize poetry even after a month's vigorous exercise in memorizing an extensive poetic work. E. L. Thorndike, with R. S. Woodworth (1901), empirically determined, in a series of experiments, that mental exercise had no significant transfer effect. It was concluded that the value of academic disciplines was inherent in the subjects themselves but not in transfer to other situations. This has great meaning for contemporary teachers. Teachers must recognize that if their subject is to have transfer value, the transfer application must be taught as well. Imaginative use of simulations can often help toward this end, as we shall see when we subsequently describe and discuss various teaching methods. Certainly transfer of specific classroom learnings to more generalized conditions should be one of the more fundamental purposes of education. For this reason, it is essential to concentrate on improved means of transfer of learning.

Motivation

Motivation—the desire to do something—can be viewed as extrinsic or intrinsic. Extrinsic motivation takes place outside the learner. A person can be prompted to learn for many reasons quite external to himself. An example is earning high grades for improved social standing with peers or parents rather than for the value of the academic subject or the ideas offered. Sometimes a person begins to learn through an extrinsically motivating factor such as compulsory class attendance and then later "becomes interested" through the efforts of a gifted, dynamic teacher or perhaps discovers that the subject is inherently more interesting than he first thought.

Intrinsic motivation is, of course, a more lasting, although perhaps a more difficult kind of motivation to obtain. It is joyful for a teacher to face students who are largely self-motivated to learn their subject. A student, intrinsically motivated, has developed the ability to plan and take responsibility for his own decisions with the absence of clear directions from above. He creates his own reward system.

Motivational conflict occurs when a person has direction toward two different goals at the same time. The conflict is easily resolved if the drive toward one goal is greater than the other. Obviously the student will move toward the goal with the greater attraction. But if both goals are equally attractive the person is said to have an approach-approach conflict. An approach-avoidance conflict exists when a particular goal has positive and negative attributes.

The teacher has often been described as "one who motivates students." Others argue that if teachers too often function as significant motivators for students, students will fail to develop critical intrinsic motivational qualities often deemed essential for autonomous persons.

The above concepts should serve as at least a basic initiation into some of the concerns teachers should have regarding student motivation. Motivational considerations will be implicit in our discussion of various teaching modalities and techniques.

Classroom Teaching Methods

There are many methods of instruction in use today. The most successful teachers seem to make use of the best elements of various teaching techniques and strategies. No one method, in and of itself, can be singled out as being better than another. The effective teacher becomes a master of a variety of techniques and uses differentiated techniques for different classes and students. Sensitive teachers are alert to the unique learning styles of various students and accommodate the type of instruction to the student.

Some of the more-common teaching approaches will be described and discussed and the usefulness and applications of each will be described. Teaching techniques range from the strictly teacher-centered to the strictly student-centered.

The Lecture Method. A straightforward teacher lecture with no provision for discussion or interruption is teacher-centered rather than student-centered. Even a textbook is less teacher-centered than a lecture because the book can be easily closed or put aside if it is not aligned with the motivational needs of the students. Probably the only defense a student has against a boring lecture is to take "time out," have one's mind wander, or stealthily read a book of particular interest. Yet the lecture method is among the most widely employed teaching techniques. And it is among the very best if its purpose is kept clear and it is well executed. Unfortunately there are too few really good lecturers. A good lecture communicates information to large or small groups with about equal success.

A good lecturer can hold the attention of his audience but even the very best lecturers can lose their audience after a period of time. Most students cannot sustain interest "marching to someone else's drummer" for an extended period of time. A teacher would be wise to learn whether he can generally sustain student interest for 40, 20, or 10 minutes at the most . . . and then *stop* lecturing at least 5 minutes before that time arises. Unfortunately, the lecture method does little to develop intrinsic motivating qualities in learners and transfer of learning values are minimal, unless the lecture is superior.

The Discussion Method. Class discussion, along with the lecture method, is one of the most popular teaching techniques. Discussion allows for both intrinsic and extrinsic motivation on the part of the students. Students, in a good discussion, have an opportunity to learn at their own rate, which is a very important factor in effective teaching. The discussion method, as with the lecture method, requires special skills on the part of the leader. Discussion techniques are often much more successful than lecture techniques for most teachers. A successful combination of lecture and discussion is the formula used by most orthodox teachers.

Recitation and Drill. This approach is useful for some aspects of learning, but it leads to a roteness seldom valued as a learning outcome. Some drill in vocabulary studies and learning of number facts may prove useful, but general usefulness is limited.

Simulations.   Simulations require a very imaginative, creative teacher. They are valuable if they closely approximate the actual condition. For example, the practice sets used in bookkeeping courses, which recreate the conditions of actual bookkeeping with check stubs, receipts, and problems all similar to the true situation, have proved extremely valuable. Simulations of moon trips for the astronauts have proved most effective in training for NASA expeditions. The transfer of learning quality is *very high* with good simulations. This is a highly useful technique in the hands of accomplished teachers. In addition to the lasting transfer advantages, students often develop important intrinsic motivation qualities, discovering for themselves goals that were not imposed by a teacher. What better need to know math than to work out a navigational chart on a highly realistic, simulated moon trip?

Confluence.   Confluent education, described by George Brown (1971) in conjunction with the Ford Esalen Project, introduces an important new approach to teaching. Confluence refers to the merger and blending of two streams—the affective (emotional) stream with the cognitive (intellectual). Certainly learning involves both the mind and the emotions, the head *and* the body. What confluent education advocates is the mixing of encounter-sensitivity techniques with academic objectives. For example, a social studies teacher, as part of a lesson on governmental budget priorities, uses encounter techniques to assist the student in coming into contact with his or her own value system or personal set of priorities. Perhaps a value clarification technique—such as involving students in choosing whether an older man or younger man be allowed to survive on a single kidney machine, requiring students to make theoretical, value-laden, difficult decisions—can lead to a more realistic understanding of the less personal issue: governmental budget priorities.

The merger of feeling and intellect often produces an exciting class, and the ideas promoted are likely to generate lasting transfer value. However, in order to conduct confluent-type classes successfully, the teacher must possess inordinate skill, special training, and a sound sense of ethics.

Games. Games, if they are simulations related to the course objectives, have much teaching value. However, if the games have no connection with the course, naturally little transfer or motivational value will be obtained.

Projects. The project method was highly refined in the Dalton Plan. In this plan the rooms of the school were arranged so that various rooms functioned as laboratories. For example, a mathematics center provides all types of learning materials with a teacher present as a resource consultant. Each assignment covers one month's time, and the assignment is called a contract. The student completes the contract, as he devised it, in his own way. This approach, with little modification, is widely used today, but the name has changed to "open classroom." The advantages of such an approach have proved significant if (1) the teachers are able to handle the wide range of interests of various students, (2) the students can be reoriented to such an open approach, and (3) the school can truly provide the necessary resources for the student to successfully complete the project. Too often all three of these essential ingredients are not present, rendering the approach much less useful.

Programmed Instruction. Programmed instruction has many merits. Programmed instruction, at one time referred to as "teaching machines," attempts to employ modern technology. Talking typewriters and computer feedback mechanisms are examples. A sound program of instruction provides for various learning styles, allowing the student to proceed at his own rate. The chief problem with programmed instruction is not with the concept. The concept is sound. The difficulty is in developing sophisticated, efficient programs. Student motivation can be maintained in a sophisticated program, but a weak program loses students. Teacher warmth, an important ingredient in the learning environment, is not usually part of programmed instruction. The weakest attribute of programmed instruction, as with many of the teaching techniques that we have discussed, is its relative inability to promote transfer of learning.

Differentiated Teaching Techniques for Individual Students and Teachers. The talented teacher will use the full range of teaching techniques, perhaps with emphasis on the use of carefully developed and lively simulations if a high degree of transfer of learning is considered significant. However, a skillful blend of the lecture method, discussion, projects, programmed instruction, and even occasional recitation or drill used discriminately can greatly assist the prospective learner and earn the teacher a good reputation with both his peers and his students. If one lectures, he should lecture well. If one leads a discussion, he should do it with finesse. If one uses a simulation, the simulation should be well organized. One should try to master all of these techniques and keep them accessible, earning the teacher a top rating on the cognitive-flexibility-rigidity continuum.

EVALUATION OF STUDENTS

Marks and Grades

The grading system has been and is the subject of continuing controversy. The fundamental question is not whether teachers should offer some feedback to students and their parents. The answer to that question is "Of course." The real question is "What form should this feedback to students take?" Certainly a pass-fail system is feedback of a sort. Will this sufficiently satisfy most students? Perhaps, but what about colleges and professional schools? Don't these schools require a more discriminating evaluation for each student? It should be pointed out that admissions requirements to most schools have opened up considerably in recent years. The A,B,C,D, and F form of grading has come to mean less than ever before. Perhaps the most meaningful and lasting kind of feedback a teacher can give a student is in a face-to-face situation that has been initiated by the student himself. We have observed that too many teachers are assigning and evaluating too many term papers that too many students didn't want to write and don't want evaluated by their instructors. Perhaps student self-evaluation, with teachers serving as resources on call when asked, is the way of the future.

Norms

It is appropriate to offer a few words about class norms at this juncture. Most educators agree that a "C" in a class of gifted math students means something quite different than a "C" in a class of average math students. If educators persist in attempting to render precise grading then they should do the job expertly, and each letter grade should also include the *norm group* that the teacher is using. For example, the grade of "C" normally equals "average," but "average" for a gifted class is "above average" for a normal class. Therefore the grade of "C" should be reported "C (for normal class in Specialtown)." Furthermore, it should be recognized that Specialtown is below average nationally and this, also, should be indicated. These descriptive measures, we all know, are seldom taken.

Tests

Tests are of two basic kinds, teacher-made and mass produced, standardized. Teacher-made tests are most often chosen to measure student achievement in subject matter. Objective and subjective essay type tests each have particular strengths and weaknesses with which the prospective teacher should become familiar.

Objective Types

Multiple choice: provides for rapid marking, standardized measure but is difficult to write. Each question should have at least four options and each option should be attractive.

Fill in: this type of test relatively easy to write and score, usually encourages rote memory on the part of the students—a major flaw.

Matching: comments similar to fill-in questions mentioned above.

Essays: relatively easy to write. Extremely difficult to evaluate in a standardized manner. In order to score properly each essay must be read independently with students name covered to eliminate bias and halo effect. Each essay is then compared with an ideal essay. The chief criticism of this type of test is that it is extremely subjective.

Achievement, Aptitude and Personality Tests

How are the outcomes of instruction evaluated? Aside from the frequently used "teacher-made" tests that we reviewed, consideration must also be given to the standardized or mass-produced achievement tests. Aptitude and personality tests will also be discussed.

Standardized Achievement Tests. Standardized or mass-produced achievement tests are usually packaged as a "test battery." For example, one achievement test includes separate tests measuring such academic areas as reading, map reading, study skills, arithmetic, social studies, and science. These separate tests, together, compose a battery.

Standardized measures of achievement are most useful; however, there are several precautions that the teacher-consumer should take;

1. Do not have faith in the composite grade-level score of an achievement test battery. A grade level norm of 5.1 indicates that a student has achieved at the fifth grade, one month level, but this grade level norm, derived by averaging the grade-level achievement found in the various achievement tests, is similar to averaging six eggs, two bananas, and four sides of beef and arriving at an average of 4.0. All subjects should not be given the same weight. Is map reading considered to have the identical significance of mathematics comprehension in the fifth grade? Few teachers would say so. Yet the composite score in achievement tests is often abusively used.

2. Do not overestimate the precision of a grade-level norm. If a student scored 5.0 at the beginning in math and at the end of the year scores 6.5, can it be accurately stated that "he grew a year and a half" in one year? The answer is "no." Often simply answering two or three more questions correctly can ad-

vance a student many months—and two or three items difference is likely part of a standard error of measurement. That is, all tests presume some error, due to chance. The grade-level norm indicator, while among the most convenient ways of reporting scores, is extremely misleading. It is best to report scores in percentiles or stanines rather than grade-level norms. A stanine, briefly, distributes scores throughout the normal curve over nine intervals, with the first stanine representing the lowest group, the fifth stanine indicating average, and the ninth stanine representing the highest or superior group. Percentiles indicate where a student is in relation to 99 other students with regard to the tested quality. For example, the 50th percentile means that half of the students fall below that score and half did better. Our point, once again, is that the use of stanines or percentiles is generally less *misleading* than the prevailing use of grade-level norms. For thorough information on norms and various achievement tests, we recommend Thorndike and Hagen's *Measurement and Evaluation in Psychology and Education.*

Various norms such as grade level, stanines, and percentiles are interchangeable. The following chart depicting the normal curve and the various norm indicators should clarify this point.

3. Do not have blind faith in achievement tests measuring social studies or science if the test items have not been checked to determine if the test measures the content of the curriculum as taught. It has not been possible to standardize science or social studies curriculums around the country and,

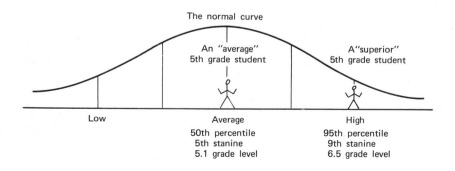

The normal curve

An "average"
5th grade student

A "superior"
5th grade student

Low

Average
50th percentile
5th stanine
5.1 grade level

High
95th percentile
9th stanine
6.5 grade level

therefore, standardized tests may not be at all appropriate in many areas. One should make a content analysis before using a standardized measure, otherwise students will be treated unfairly.

Reliability and Validity

Two important concepts to master regarding all tests are reliability and validity. Briefly, reliability raises the question of whether the test measures the same substance with a reasonable degree of regularity. For example, if I gave a reading achievement test today and a similar version of the same test tomorrow, and the students performed similarly on both tests, I could safely say that the test was reliable. If the students performed quite differently from one test administration to the next, I would say that the test was unreliable; that is, I could not trust it. Certainly teachers want trustworthy test results and therefore should always attempt to determine if a test is reliable.

Perhaps even more important is the question Is the test valid? That is, does the test measure what it purports to measure? Achievement tests are usually valid. Math tests tend to measure math achievement, reading tests tend to measure reading achievement, and so on. However, the question of the validity of aptitude and personality tests is a bit less reassuring.

Aptitude Tests

Aptitude tests, tests that attempt to predict how a student will perform in the future, are also of great interest and use to teachers. Aptitudes for certain kinds of work and various subjects are often assessed through tests. Usually aptitude tests are really achievement tests, based on the assumption that the best prediction of future performance can be based on past performance.

The best predictor of how a student will perform in English Eight is often answered by knowing how he performed in English Seven. There are several pitfalls teachers should be aware of with regard to aptitude tests, particularly measures of scholastic aptitude popularly misnomered "IQ tests."

IQ or Intelligence Tests

These tests do *not* measure general intelligence but instead, scholastic aptitude. They correlate well with indicators of success in school. But success in school is only one fraction of life. General intelligence is composed of such factors as creativity and social qualities. So-called "IQ Tests" do not measure these qualities and are, therefore, misnomers. They should rightfully be referred to as scholastic ability tests since they are reasonably good predictors of how one will succeed in school. Most of these tests (individual or group) have a satisfactory degree of reliability and validity. Little success has been reported in efforts to develop a "culture-free" test measuring scholastic ability. Their greatest weakness is the white middle-class bias usually built into the test items.

Personality Tests

Teachers must be extremely careful not to have undue faith in tests measuring personality traits. Though they have a great deal of clinical value in the counseling of a student (mainly for providing clues worthy of further inquiry) personality tests generally are extremely *unreliable* and often have low *validity* coefficients.

Here we reviewed concepts and research bearing on both learning and teaching. We explored various teaching methodologies and examined issues regarding grading and testing. The three selections that follow highlight the learning-teaching process, classroom control and management, and the evaluation of instruction. We expect that the issues emanating from these cases will provoke you to return to portions of this essay for rereading.

Theme 6 The Teaching Process

The question What is effective teaching? is far more difficult to answer than one would imagine. Some critics have taken issue with the emphasis usually given to teaching processes, urging instead that greater attention be given to learners and learning processes. "Certainly much learning takes place without teachers and, in many instances, in spite of teachers," these critics argue. After 27 years of classroom teaching, the teacher in the subsequent portrayal reviews some of the dramatic changes that have transpired in his particular efforts toward "effective teaching."

Selection 6 GOOD TEACHING

Teacher: Donald Barker
Age: 51
Experience: 27 years, elementary and secondary

It's difficult to reconcile the fact that over 25 years ago, as I recall, I was totally convinced that I was most certainly among the very best teachers in these United States, and now, a quarter of a century later, I am not even sure that I know what that process we call teaching really is. But, oh, I was so very certain then.

You see, my premise was ultrasimplistic. I was honestly convinced, somehow, that if I was very energetic and absolutely enthusiastic about my subject matter (which happened to be social studies) and, most importantly, if I held forth and discussed, most lucidly, the subject at hand, that indeed I would be doing a perfectly marvelous job of teaching. After all, I reasoned, most of my colleagues were not nearly as articulate or enthusiastic as I was. Certainly I was a far cry from the stereotyped old fashioned schoolmarm with her dull, unimaginative, assign-study-recite approach.

My classroom control was excellent. Jack Simms, my department chairman who observed my classes from time to time, wrote in his reports that he was very impressed. The students seemed attentive, well behaved, and I, perhaps even more than anyone, was enjoying the resonance of my voice about the room. Of course, five periods a day of that became to be a bit much after a few years. However, I was a stoic, loyal to my work, and continued energetically to hold forth day after day after day.

I don't recall when the turning point came, or even if there was a particular turning point. I suppose it was just very gradually. Somehow, I began to wonder, even though I was from all appearances, at least, succeeding to entertain, even mesmorize some of my classes, I began to wonder if I was in fact really accomplishing anything truly worthwhile. "Was I teaching? Were my students really learning—and more important, *what* were they learning?"

My fundamental question I suppose, concerned the nature of their motivation. It seemed to me that I was quite effective in motivating students to learn about social studies. But then came the question, "Is that really my job—that of motivating them to learn social studies?" No question that for years I was proceeding on that premise. Of course. Yet, the thought struck me, these youngsters sit back in my classes with the attitude, "O.K. teach, motivate me into learning about social studies, that's what you're being paid for, fella!" And then it dawned on me, "Yes, young man, I'm supposed to be your supreme academic motivator, and you have become very dependent all through school on motivators like me, and a whole lot of motivators *outside* of yourself. "When, may I ask, are you going to start motivating yourself, *by yourself,* if ever?" When?

You and I have by and large produced an extremely docile, sheeplike mass of young people through the good auspices of our schools. "When," I asked myself, "am I going to begin to help these youngsters in my classes begin to develop a sense of self, a sense of creating one's own destiny? What could I do to help them from being passive, docile, easily managed—and manipulated? What could I do to help them to begin to take responsibility for themselves—to become their own man, so to speak?"

When these kinds of questions took hold in my mind, I began to get my first major doubts about my professional competency. Oh certainly, I was an entertainer par excellence. But a great teacher? Far from it. In fact, was I a teacher, in the best sense of the word, at all?

Yes, I thought I was a master teacher after the first few years teaching. I figured that I had overcome the mistakes most new, young, idealistic teachers make, like being a bit too informal with the kids, first names, too much buddy-buddy, and all that. And then I knew that many students loved me and even my principal was said to admire my work. But now, after all these years I find I'm not even sure what teaching is, or even if there is such a thing as teaching.

Sometimes, when I think too much, I come to the opinion that there really is no such thing at all as teaching . . . just learners and learning, so called, if teachers stay out of their way.

Why then, you ask, have I continued all these years if I have so many doubts about what I'm doing? I don't know. I don't really know. . . .

Suggestions for Further Study

1. Donald Barker contends that he was not an effective teacher during his early years as a teacher. In your opinion, is his definition of good teaching too narrow or severe? What is an acceptable definition of teaching? What are the necessary ingredients in effective teaching? Support your position, as best as you can.
2. Compare the relative merits of intrinsic and extrinsic motivation in learning. Illustrate.
3. Locate several classroom teachers that have been identified by principals, students, or others as highly effective. Interview these teachers and see if you can ascertain traits and characteristics common to all of them.
4. To what extent do you equate good teaching with entertainment? React to the statement "Learning should be fun."
5. What personal characteristics and qualities do you possess that should stand you in good stead as a teacher? What aspects of yourself do you have yet to develop in order to achieve your maximum potential as a teacher?
6. To what extent do you think differently about teaching than Donald Barker does? Explain. Do you agree, as Barker suggests, that there is in fact, no such thing as teaching, only learning? Discuss.

Theme 7 Classroom Management

New teachers are confronted with the always unromantic requisites of basic housekeeping: roll taking, class registers, preparation of teaching materials, requisition of supplies, and, of course, the most significant essential, "good classroom control." Part of the folklore that the new teacher inevitably encounters is the oversimplified maxim "Don't smile until Thanksgiving!" In some schools, the warning "Don't smile at all" has become the byword. Martin Graham, an old timer, laments for "the good old days of corporal punishment" and contrasts those days with modern-day "psychological" approaches.

Selection 7 A TOUGH ROW

Teacher: Martin Graham
Age: 64
Experience: 41 years, secondary

Listen, kids want to be disciplined. They still want someone to lean on, they still want to be told. But the trouble with this school is that both the teachers *and* the administration are afraid of the kids. They're running scared. The kids are managing them instead of them managing the kids. It is a disgusting and frightening thing to see.

And the kids, they don't like it either, believe me. Oh, they'll take advantage all right and I can't blame them for that. You'd take advantage too if you were in their position, wouldn't you? But deep down inside, they resent it. They can sense that it's not right. Adults abdicating their responsibility to kids, coddling them, psychoanalyzing them half to death. It's sickening.

Oh, it wasn't always that way here. Not too many years ago in this very school, if a kid stepped out of line the teacher would smack him right across the face. That's right. Right across the chops. And if the kid were to say, like today, "I'll sue you," then the teacher would say, "Go right ahead and sue me young fella, but I'm afraid I'm all out of sue money just now!" And then he would smack him once again just for having had the audacity to act that way.

Parents upset? Oh no, not in those days. In those days the parents would support you. And the administration too. Many is the father that called me and said, "Look, Mr. Graham, see what you can do with him. He's not easy to handle. We have difficulty with him at home so I know that he's not easy to control in school!" Then they

107

would say, "Do what you have to Mr. Graham. Do what you have to. We can't shape him up, maybe you can, Mr. Graham." Now that's what I call parent support. And believe me it helped, and I was able to shape up quite a few youngsters, and it was mutually appreciated.

But even without parent support, there were ways. You see, you had the support of the administration in those days. We had ways to handle a kid that no one could question. Like little playful nobbies with the knuckles on the top of the head, in the hair where it didn't show. And always given with a smile, so the kid wasn't brought into a direct confrontation.

Oh listen, this little corporal punishment wasn't half as bad as it's made out to be. In fact, the very fact that you were able to use it made life in the classroom more humane for everyone—for the other kids, for the teacher and yes, even for the kid being punished. You hardly ever had to use it because there was fear. The kids knew you could use it if necessary. See what I mean?

Now, the books all say, I know, be sensitive to the child's problems. Make sure the work is interesting. Keep the children totally busy all day. If a child acts up, search yourself and see what you are doing wrong. Check with the child's guidance counselor. Is everything all right at home? Does he have hobbies, playtime, friends? How is his poor psyche? Has he received or is he receiving psychotherapy? Frankly, that's all gobbledygook.

Oh, that soft-hearted, soft-headed approach would be fine if it worked. But look at the condition of our schools today, and all with the permissive approach dominant, too. Believe me, do not rely on the wisdom of the guidance counselor or the school psychologists if a kid in your class is a discipline problem. Rely on yourself.

Above all, don't send anybody to the principal's office. It will count against you. There's only one person to rely on and that is yourself. And without corporal punishment, believe me, you've got a tough row to hoe, my friend, a tough row to hoe.

Suggestions for Further Study

1. Identify some of the key issues in this selection and when appropriate, examine each of these issues with regard to the following:

(a) ethical considerations

(b) basic philosophical assumptions

(c) pragmatic factors

2. Trace the history of corporal punishment in American schools. Are there currently any states in the United States that give approval to limited use of such a method of discipline? What is your position regarding effective means of classroom discipline?

3. Classroom management and control are important factors for all teachers. Interview a number of experienced classroom teachers who are reputed to have sound classroom management practices. Compare their philosophies and practices.

4. Supervisors, counselors, and psychologists are sometimes able to offer help with classroom management. Locate and interview some of these consultants. In what way are their suggestions similar or different from the teachers that you interviewed in No. 3 above.

5. What broad psychological and social trends infringe upon successful classroom management? Cite sources for your observations.

Theme 8 Evaluation of Instruction

At least once, and sometimes several times each academic year, a supervisor of instruction, the principal, or some other official "visits" the classroom teacher to evaluate the quality of the teacher's work. This ritual is often followed by a conference in which the supervisor and teacher mutually review the observation report. There is still controversy as to what represents an effective teaching approach. In recent years, students' views have been seriously considered as part of the evaluation process. With greater emphasis today on "accountability" and "performance assessment" for teachers, the evaluation checklist has become a serious and crucial evaluation device. Dena Grant reviews her classes' recent evaluation of her work in the selection that follows.

Selection 8   THANKS LARGELY TO MR. FREY

Teacher: Dena Grant
Age: 22
Experience: 2 years, secondary

Dena was relieved when she reviewed her classes' evaluation of her teaching ability. On a five-point scale where 1 is lowest and 5 represents the highest possible score, she was rated average or better in *almost* every quality. The 20 characteristics on the form were divided into four major categories; teacher-student relations, teaching methods and techniques, teacher's evaluation procedures and, finally, an overall or general rating.

Dena was especially proud that she was rated highest by her students in her ability to engage her class in critical thinking. "This is probably the most important aspect of my work as a teacher," she contended.

There was one area in which she received a low score. That was in terms of her tolerance toward different points of view. She thought it unfortunate that this is considered an important quality for a teacher to possess. "It's just that I cannot accept random, unjustified opinions. Oh, I can accept an opinion if it has been carefully reasoned and well thought out but not a capricious, unthinking view. I haven't the patience or the tolerance for that. Too bad that counts against me on this form. I think that's unfair."

Another part of the evaluation form disturbed Dena—the statement "Course plans and objectives are always carefully developed in advance." She had been taught, and firmly believed, that a really good teacher should be spontaneous. Her philosophy was to develop the course in conjunction *with* the class, not independently *for* the

111

class. Judging from the below-average rating she received, Dena suspected that the students did not quite commiserate with her position.

However, as she reviewed her above-average overall rating of teaching ability she mused, "Not bad, really. Not bad." She was glad that her students seemed to respect her work as a teacher. "I know that there is no absolutely objective way to measure the quality of my teaching, but at least this is an effort at objectivity," she thought.

"But somehow," Dena lamented, "something is out of kilter with this effort too. Teaching is much, much more than what they are attempting to measure here. Even if my students were to think I was perfect in every respect, would this still mean that I was a good teacher? After all, some of the best teachers I had when I was in school were those that I least appreciated at the time. It wasn't until years later that I realized what they had helped me learn." She thought of Mr. Frey, her high school Spanish teacher. "We all hated him when he pressured us so much. His class was so difficult. But now, seven years later, I'm finally starting to appreciate what a marvelous teacher he was. At least now, I can *speak* Spanish, thanks largely to Mr. Frey. Isn't that the true measure of a Spanish teacher?"

Suggestions for Further Study

1. There have been a number of efforts to assess the performance of classroom teachers. What evidence can you cite that supports the inclusion of specific traits or conpetencies on a teacher-rating scale? What means would you suggest to more effectively evaluate instruction?

2. Examine several rating scales used in various school districts to evaluate classroom teachers. What do these scales have in common? Do these scales appear to measure with any degree of accuracy the competency of teachers? What is a competent teacher? Discuss.

3. In conjunction with one of your classmates, secure permis-

sion to visit several classrooms. Observe the instruction and attempt to describe and evaluate the teacher's performance. What criteria for evaluation will you use? Are these defensible criteria? Discuss. Compare your observation findings with those of your classmates. In what way did you differ? Why?

4. Form a panel composed of a teacher, a student, a classroom supervisor, and a guidance counselor. Have them react to the selection "Thanks Largely to Mr. Frey." Contrast their views and opinions. In what way do their perspectives differ?

Annotated Bibliography

Bigge, Morris L. *Learning Theory for Teachers* (2nd ed.). New York: Harper and Row, 1971. The major families of contemporary learning theory are systematically reviewed. Bigge clarifies the relationship between learning and teaching.

Brown, George Isaac. *Human Teaching for Human Learning: An Introduction to Confluent Education*. New York: The Viking Press, 1971. The principles of confluent education; the blending of the affective and cognitive domains are described, and useful classroom procedures enumerated. The emphasis is on a more humanistic education process in the classroom.

Bruner, Jerome S. *Toward a Theory of Instruction*. New York: W. W. Norton & Co., 1968. Bruner, drawing from actual situations, examines children's learning processes and derives a number of key principles on which to base instruction.

Bugelski, Bergen Richard. *The Psychology of Learning Applied to Teaching* (2nd ed.). New York: The Bobbs-Merrill Co., 1971. This book focuses on practical information for classroom teachers and relies on a minimum of theory. Specific advice and procedures are detailed, drawing on various aspects of educational psychology.

Highet, Gilbert. *The Art of Teaching*. New York: Alfred Knopf, 1958. A language and literature professor writes interestingly about teaching based largely on his personal reflections. He also reviews the teaching approaches of acknowledged great teachers from Socrates to the present day.

Jackson, Phillip W. *Life in Classrooms*. New York: Holt, Rinehart and Winston, 1968. Emphasis is on elementary classrooms and what goes on in them. Based partly on Jackson's observations in several first- and second-grade classrooms, the text focuses on the classroom as an unusual social system.

Kuethe, James L. *The Teaching-Learning Process*. Glenview, Illinois: Scott, Foresman and Co., 1968. This is a concise, soundly conceived and developed text that offers a clear, straightforward introduction to the theory and principles underlying teaching and learning.

Rogers, Carl R. *Freedom to Learn*. Columbus, Ohio: Charles E. Merrill, 1969. Rogers, whose positions we described in the preceding essay, brings together his divergent writings on education and includes closely related views of selected others; all chapters advance the "freedom to learn" concept.

Section IV   THE TEACHER

This introduction is devoted to an examination of American public-school teachers—who they are, their supply-and-demand trends, the kind of preparation they must have for teaching, and some of the problems they face as practitioners.

WHO THEY ARE

The American public-school teacher is a member of the largest professional group in the United States. Figures for the school year 1971–1972, indicate that 2,089,623 persons were employed as classroom teachers:

1.   Of the total, approximately two-thirds are women and one-third are men.

2.   The proportion of elementary to secondary teachers is 52.6 percent to 47.4 percent.

3.   Approximately 60 percent are under age 39.

4.   Only 28.2 percent of them teach in large school districts with enrollments of more than 25,000.

5.   Politically, 60.5 percent view themselves as either strongly or moderately conservative.

6.   Regarding religious affiliation, 78.3 percent are members of an organized church or synagogue.

(NEA Research, Vol. 50, 1972)

TEACHER SUPPLY AND DEMAND

The 1950s and 1960s witnessed an unprecedented rise in pupil enrollments and, concomitantly, a demand for additional teachers. The 1970s is, however, quite unlike previous periods. We are beginning to experience a decline in pupil enrollments that, when projected over the next several years, will affect the demand for new teachers. Enrollment for the 1970–1971 school year over the 1971–1972 school year has, in fact, declined at the elementary level from 28,109,090 to 28,069,411 for a loss of 39,679 pupils. Projected enrollments at the secondary level are expected to drop from the present 18.6 million to approximately 14.3 million over the coming decade. Undoubtedly, there will be a diminished demand for additional teachers over the next several years. However, the overall picture is not quite as bleak as the previous data indicate. During the 1950s and 1960s, when demand exceeded supply, many teachers were hired who had attained minimum preparation. Many are still teaching in areas for which they are not fully qualified. For example, during the year 1970–1971, 15.2 percent of teachers nationwide were teaching 50 percent or more time outside their major field of preparation (NEA Research, Vol. 50, 1972). The National Education Association Research Division estimated that 301,027 persons completed teacher preparation programs but that their Quality Criterion Estimate showed a need for 446,500 teachers to provide fully competent people in all subject areas. There was, therefore, an excess of demand over supply for 145,473 teachers (NEA, 1970).

Another source of demand for new teachers is the replacements for persons leaving the profession. In 1970–1971, for example, there was a need for 88,800 new elementary teachers and 77,300 secondary teachers resulting from teacher loss. In percentages, these figures reflect approximately an 8 percent teacher turnover rate (NEA, 1970).

Combining the two sets of data that indicate declining enrollments with the need for better-qualified personnel, we will probably experience a new kind of supply-and-demand situation where only persons with the highest credentials will be considered as replacements for teachers leaving the profession.

PROFESSIONAL PROBLEMS

In this section several areas of concern dealing with various professional aspects of teaching will be discussed. Included are certification, salary, policies, tenure, grievance, grievance procedures, and retirement systems.

Admission to the Profession-Certification

All states require that teachers obtain a license, certificate or permit to teach, giving legal sanction to teach. Requirements for obtaining a license vary widely among the states. A large proportion accept completion of an approved college program as satisfactory preparation for certification, while some states have a prescribed curriculum that must be completed to obtain the license. Forty-eight states and the District of Columbia require completion of the Bachelor's degree. Nebraska and South Dakota each require completion of 60 semester hours (Woellner, 1972).

There is a wide range of types of certificates issued by the states. Some states issue a single standard or life certificate valid for an indefinite period. Other states issue either two or three levels of certificates based on college training and/or years of teaching experience. In some cases there are renewals at 5- or 10-year intervals, or they are renewable at the beginning levels and are permanent at the higher levels. Still other states offer only renewable certificates at varying intervals of from 1 year to 10 years.

Members of the profession have debated several aspects of the certification process including the academic and performance requirements, the time validity of licenses, whether certification exams should be required, and the role of practicing teachers in the certification process.

Academic Requirements for Certification

Data stated previously indicate that a four year Bachelor's degree is a minimum requirement for certification. For the years ahead, the National Commission on Teacher Education and Professional Standards of the NEA have long recommended a fifth-year level of preparation for continuing or permanent certification (NEA, 1964).

There is underway, at present, a movement away from college preparatory programs as the major criterion for certification towards a competency-based approach to certification. Under such curricula a candidate would be required to complete specific classroom experiences and then apply the skills developed in actual school settings. In these programs, certification would be based on competence in performing certain specified skills in on-the-job settings, rather than completion of prescribed course of study. New York, Texas, and Utah are presently experimenting with such programs.

Time Validity of State Licenses

Unlike the medical or law professions where a person is certified as competent at the completion of his preparatory training, some states issue licenses valid only for specified periods, such as 5 years or 10 years. This practice has been questioned by the professionals who argue that teachers should receive the same status in the licensing process as other professions. On the other hand, some persons argue that parents do not have the opportunity to evaluate the efficiency of teachers and, therefore, the state should do so, mainly by issuing renewable certificates based on competence and professional growth.

Certification Exams

Another issue relative to the certification process concerns the need for certification exams that purport to certify knowledge and skills acquired during the preparatory period. There has been a tendency in recent years to eliminate such tests on the basis that they tend to standardize teacher-training programs thereby discouraging uniqueness and creativity. Notwithstanding the problems related to such exams, some larger cities and several states still require passage of a standardized test as a requisite for obtaining a teaching license.

Role of Practitioners in the Licensing Process

Teachers have been exerting greater influence in professional matters over the past several years. One area of involvement has been a demand for a measure of control over the certification process. Where traditionally the licensing procedure has been shared between the various universities and the states, the movement underway at present is for a tripartite arrangement among members of the profession or their representatives, the cooperating universities, and the state. Representatives from the profession may come from regional teacher associations or where union support predominates—the regional teacher union. Such procedures are being tried experimentally in New York State where at least 14 trial projects involving tripartite certification are underway.

Salary Policies

Unlike other professions, the teacher derives almost all of her income from tax revenues, over half of which are collected at the local level. Of the total revenue receipts of $46,644,623,000 received in 1971–1972, $24,276,080,000 came from local communities. The next largest share, $19,062,-863,000 was levied by the states. Because education is a public function that is supported through taxation, salaries have generally been below those for private industry. For example, in 1971–1972 the average salary for beginning teachers with a Bachelor's degree was $7061 or 26 percent below the $9543 starting salary for persons employed in private industry. Low salaries have, in many instances, forced teachers to seek additional income during the school year and over the summer months. In 1971, 80.9 percent of the men teachers earned additional monies over and above their base salaries. For women teachers the figure was over 44 percent. The amounts of additional income earned by men and women respectively totaled

$1899 and $1076. The matter of salaries, therefore, is a significant area of concern by teachers (NEA, 1964).

TENURE

Another equally sensitive area for teachers is tenure. Historically, tenure came into being as a measure of providing regular employment for a group of predominantly itinerant teachers. As the country changed from a rural to an urban society, the need for regular full-time teachers grew proportionately. Tenure was offered as a means of keeping teachers who were paid very low wages for the services rendered. Over the years the idea of tenure has grown to where today 41 states and the District of Columbia have adopted tenure on almost a statewide basis, and another four states have continuing contracts. Six states have annual or long-term contracts. A breakdown for each category is given below (NEA, No. R-11, 1972).

1. *States with Tenure Laws*

Alabama	Iowa	[d] New York
Alaska	Kentucky	North Carolina
Arizona	Louisiana	North Dakota
Arkansas	Maine	Ohio
[a] California	Maryland	Oklahoma
Colorado	Massachusetts	Pennsylvania
[b] Connecticut	Michigan	Rhode Island
Delaware	Minnesota	South Dakota
District of Columbia	Missouri	Tennessee
[c] Florida	Montana	Virginia
Hawaii	Nevada	Washington
Idaho	New Hampshire	West Virginia
Illinois	New Jersey	Wyoming
Indiana	New Mexico	

[a] *Optional in districts with an average attendance under 250 people.*

[b] *Special tenure laws govern certain cities.*

[c] *Special local tenure laws govern certain counties.*

[d] *Certain rural districts not covered.*

2. *States with Continuing Contract of Spring Notification Type* (less than statewide exceptions are noted)

Kansas   Kansas City, Topeka, and Wichita
Nebraska   Lincoln and Omaha
Oregon   Districts with an average daily attendance of 4500 or more, and districts where tenure was in effect on August 24, 1965
Wisconsin   County and city of Milwaukee

3. *Annual or Long-Term Contracts*

Georgia   (except for De Valk, Fulton, and Richmond counties)
Mississippi
South Carolina   (status silent on permissible length of contract term)
Utah   ″
Vermont   ″

The issue of tenure has been widely debated by persons inside and outside the profession. Proponents of tenure argue that it stimulates better classroom instruction by providing emotional security for teachers, and it removes the need for the political maneuvering that would occur if teachers were dependent on another kind of reappointment system. Those against tenure argue that classroom instruction can suffer where incompetent teachers acquire tenure or when teachers for one reason or another lose their effectiveness in the classroom. Since 82 percent of the states presently have tenure laws in effect, the security-effectiveness model that tenure provides versus another kind of system is difficult to test accurately.

Additional insights on how the issue of tenure affects the individual teacher are offered in Selection 15, "He Didn't Belong Here." This interesting case deals with the question of whether or not to grant tenure to a teacher and how several factors affected the final decision.

The matter of grievance procedures has received increasing support among teachers. A survey conducted by the National Education Association in 1966–1967 and 1967–1968 shows a

55.8 percent increase in grievance procedures by local school districts (NEA, 1969). Of the agreements in effect, two broad categories were identified. The first is termed "procedural" because it simply delineates procedures for initiating and conducting a grievance. The second type, called a "comprehensive agreement," not only states procedure but also includes specific items such as salaries and fringe benefits. In the same study by the NEA in which 7175 school districts in all 50 states and the District of Columbia were polled and responses were obtained from 6352 districts, all states except Alabama, Georgia, Hawaii, and Louisiana reported some form of grievance procedures. Of the agreements in effect, 2212 or approximately 35 percent percent were procedural and 603 or 10 percent were comprehensive agreements. The following 17 states reported the latter type in effect in some districts:

Colorado	Massachusetts	Pennsylvania
Connecticut	Michigan	Rhode Island
District of Columbia	Montana	Virginia
Illinois	New Jersey	Washington
Indiana	New York	Wisconsin
Maryland	Ohio	

An interesting facet of the grievance procedure is the provision for third-party assistance outside the school in settling disputes. Of the comprehensive agreements in effect, 83 percent provide for outside assistance for the last step or final appeal. The parties most often selected to act as third parties are the state public employee or labor board (40 percent) and the American Arbitration Association (45 percent). The remaining agreements call for parties named in the agreements, persons jointly selected by the parties, the State Commissioner of Education, the United States Mediation and Conciliation Service, or persons from other categories not previously specified.

In view of the present trend in grievance procedures, it does appear that many of the areas affecting teacher welfare will be negotiated between teachers and Boards of Education with outside assistance if needed rather than mandated by Boards of Education with teachers performing only advisory functions.

The effects of professional organizations upon the individual teacher are discussed in Selection 14, "Just a Matter of Time." In this case the personal feelings of teachers are presented with regard to complicated decisions facing a teacher.

RETIREMENT SYSTEMS

Another aspect of teacher concern is retirement systems. Laws related to retirement are not often discussed with teachers, and it is, therefore, important for teachers to become acquainted with the various benefits provided under existing statutes. As with certification, laws vary considerably from state to state. Generally, however, retirement systems are categorized into two broad types. First, there are statewide teachers' systems covering only teachers. The second type is called a statewide public employees system to which teachers belong. Included in this latter category are other civil servants such as state and municipal employees. Thirty-six states have special teacher retirement systems, while 14 states have statewide public employee systems. A second important feature of the various retirements is the provision for Social Security coverage. At present, 14 states have no provision for such coverage for teachers. They are:

Alaska	Illinois	Missouri
California	Kentucky	Nevada
Colorado	Louisiana	Ohio
Connecticut	Maine	Rhode Island
Florida	Massachusetts	

Retirement systems vary considerably in terms of specific provisions relative to such items as membership, creditable service, withdrawals and refunds, members' borrowing, vesting retirement requirements, death benefits, survivor benefits, financing, and administration of the system. Generally members are given the option to retire between the ages of 55 and 65 depending on state laws. Some states have two benefits paid to retirees: a pension for a specified amount and an annuity based on sex and length of service and monies contributed. Still other states permit membership in a supplemental annuity such as TIAA (Teachers Insurance and Annuity), while others restrict membership to a single system. Contributions into the system by a participating member and the local school and benefits paid to retirees vary greatly from state to state.

Over a normal teaching career the participating member pays a large sum of money into his retirement system and he should become familiar with the specific provisions and the extent of coverage he has while teaching. It is unfortunate that states do not make a greater effort to keep teachers up-to-date concerning details of the laws governing retirement systems as well as an up-to-date accounting of one's accumulated contributions.

The foregoing discussion dealt with the more definitive and formalized problems which teachers encounter. Now the personal relationships of teacher vis à vis colleagues and administrators will be presented. Problem areas include the beginning teacher, job satisfaction, teacher-teacher relationships, and teacher-administrative relationships (NEA, Teacher Retirement, 1972).

THE BEGINNING TEACHER

The beginning teacher faces several difficult adjustments in role definition and function. First, there is the shift from student to teacher. Where she was in a subordinate position taking her direction from her teachers, she now has become *the teacher* and must direct rather than follow. She must teach rather than learn. She must plan for her students rather than carry out someone else's plans. She must make decisions rather than have most decisions made for her. For the most part she is alone directing her class rather than being a member of a class or group. Where her academic achievement weighed heavily as a measure of success in the past, her performance is what counts in the classroom. She must act rather than react.

Second, there is the matter of adjusting to her students. Will they like her? How will she balance the necessary freedom to learn with the need to maintain order? How will she adjust to students with backgrounds quite different from her own? Administrators and fellow teachers can help alleviate these anxieties on the part of the beginning teacher. Sometimes the "buddy system" is quite effective in this regard. Under such an arrangement an experienced teacher is assigned to help the novice when problems arise. Administrators too, can help the beginning teacher by maintaining an "open door" policy so that problems can be discussed openly in a spirit of cooperation.

Another concern of the beginning teacher has to do with the curriculum and methods of teaching. Will she be able to choose the right material that is academically appropriate and at the same time relevant to her students' needs? Will she be able to develop a variety of teaching strategies including proper utilization of the newer technological aids? Will she be able to strike a balance between flexibility and chaos in classroom management?

A fourth type of problem for the new teacher is that of developing mutually satisfying relationships with her colleagues. In the daily routine of teaching there really is very little time for developing and maintaining meaningful communication with other teachers. At lunch time and faculty meetings time is short and the setting is usually inappropriate for such contacts. However, small-group committee work and one-to-one conversations at the end of the day can prove quite helpful in establishing rapport with one's colleagues.

Another area in which a teacher can gain personal satisfaction is by keeping an open mind toward innovations in education and demonstrating a willingness to try new ideas. In this way she can utilize her creative abilities and perhaps add a new dimension to her teaching. She may discover new techniques that can help her in reaching one or more of her students, thereby feeling a sense of accomplishment that she would not have gained otherwise.

Teacher-training institutions can go a long way in easing the transition of student to teacher by providing realistic simulations and on-the-job experiences that give apprentice teachers an opportunity to test their capabilities in actual classroom settings. In Selection 2, "Teacher Education Has a Long Way to Go," one is exposed to some of the shortcomings of teacher education and the ways in which the curriculum can be made more meaningful for students.

In summary, then, the new teacher is faced with problems of dramatic proportions. Having to transform herself from student to teacher, dealing with perhaps several classes of new students, maintaining a healthy classroom atmosphere, teaching material appropriate to the students' needs, and gaining recognition from her peers are all substantial areas with which the new teacher needs the cooperation and assistance of the school staff.

JOB SATISFACTION

The teacher who begins her career after college and continues to retirement devotes about 35 years to her work. By any measure that is a very long time to spend at any given task. Rarely in this time does she spend more than 180 days with any one group of youngsters. Her class is only one in the normal 13-year life span of her students. At the secondary level she is one teacher out of several that the student has in a given day. She is assigned her class and must do her best to help each child to the best of her ability. By and large the curriculum is prescribed either by state regulations or local mandate. How does she achieve satisfaction in teaching within these limitations? For many persons the limitations outweigh the rewards, and they strive to receive other assignments outside the classroom such as guidance counselors, administrators, or other staff positions. Still others leave the profession entirely. The truly dedicated teacher then, has to develop or enjoy something within the realm of teaching that usually is related to, using Eric Fromm's phrase, the "art of giving." She must be willing to give of herself physically and emotionally, even though in many cases she cannot get immediate satisfaction for her efforts. She must realize that youngsters, even though they may not express it explicitly, need her special attention and help in the process of growing up. Herein lies the key to job satisfaction: knowing that students need your professional guidance and being able to give of yourself to fulfill these needs. This act of giving is perhaps the only self-generating force that provides continuing job satisfaction for the teacher. Other factors, such as grade-level assignments and physical setting may be important in minor and transitional ways but are not overriding concerns over the long terms.

Selection 10, "Paper Marking Automation," describes one of the areas of possible frustration on the part of teachers and what can happen when the marking of papers is perceived as an overwhelming task in itself.

TEACHER-TEACHER RELATIONSHIPS

Related to job satisfaction is the level of esteem that teachers enjoy with their colleagues. Long-term relationships with a variety of people are, at best, difficult to maintain. Teachers are not of a single type or personality; they usually have very diverse personal qualities. Thus, it takes a special effort for a teacher to maintain healthy relationships with all or most of her coworkers. A prerequisite of course, is for the teacher to be a secure, self-actualizing person who can be open in her dealings with others. These attributes provide a basis for sharing of ideas and experiences that are essential to developing and sustaining long-term personal and professional relationships.

Teachers can extend themselves to their colleagues by volunteering to work on cooperative projects. One has, perhaps, often heard the old cliche "never volunteer" but, in reality, quite the opposite is true. Joining with others gives an opportunity to participate and demonstrate capabilities. If these new ventures are successful they tend to further enhance the teacher's professional status vis à vis the rest of the faculty.

Still another and quite obvious way to gain the respect of one's colleagues is to be successful in teaching. The cliche says that nothing succeeds like success. In teaching this is an important factor. Successful teaching, which is the central task of the school, gains the admiration and respect of all who are concerned with education: the students, teachers, administrators, and parents. It gives the teacher the security and confidence to extend herself with her colleagues.

In summary, then, teacher-teacher relationships are dependent on several factors: one's own personality, success in the classroom, a willingness to participate in the affairs of the school, and an openness toward innovation and creativity in the school's program.

In Selection 12, "Blake's Last Rite," we are exposed to a situation where, for a variety of reasons, poor interpersonal relations led to the demise rather than enhancement of the teacher's professional development.

TEACHER-ADMINISTRATOR RELATIONSHIPS

The administrator sets the tone for the school. Within a matter of weeks his influence, either real or perceived, can be felt throughout the school. If it is a positive democratic administration, then the successful teachers should have little difficulty gaining the respect and recognition they deserve. If, on the other hand, teachers are faced with an apathetic, self-seeking or incompetent administration, then they are faced with a frustrating situation. Little of the creative work they are doing is recognized, appreciated, or rewarded, and their personal satisfaction is similarly diminished.

In Selection 13, "Don't Rock Frank Corey's Boat," we experience the frustration of a teacher who is faced with an indifferent and apathetic administration.

In this introduction, we discussed a wide range of issues that teachers must deal with. Some trends are appearing, as in the area of supply and demand for new teachers where a leveling off and a decline in enrollments can be predicted for the next decade. Salaries have improved considerably over the past decade but are well below comparable positions in private industry. There has been a dramatic increase in the number of school districts having grievance procedures in operation, thus bringing under collective bargaining many areas directly affecting teachers, such as salary and fringe benefits, which heretofore had been bilaterally agreed on between the teachers and local boards of education. One of the areas where teachers need more frequent and up-to-date information is retirement. All too often teachers are not presented interpretations and implications of existing laws so that they can plan for their retirement years intelligently.

The special problems of beginning teachers were also discussed. It was recommended that teacher-training institutions modify their preparatory programs to include more simulation and on-the-job experiences for persons who plan to teach. This will help ease the transition in roles from student to teacher.

The issue of job satisfaction is a crucial one in education. Teaching has many aspects that are unique and, consequently, affect one's level of satisfaction. Cited on the positive side was the need, meaningfulness, and reward gained from teaching youngsters, while on the negative side are the limitations of class composition, curriculum, and the ability to maintain a high level of performance over a sustained period of time. Cooperative teacher-teacher and teacher-administrator relationships require a special effort on the part of both teachers and administrators. Teachers should keep an open mind toward innovations and volunteer for new projects in which they can demonstrate their abilities. Administrators should serve as catalysts in unleashing the creative potential of their staffs. If both teacher and administrator can agree that improving the learning processes of children is their central task, then perhaps many of their problems can be seen in perspective.

Theme 9 Teaching as a Career

Persons who have systematically examined the processes involved in choosing a career have observed that, contrary to the popular misconception, most people at some time preceding adulthood, simply do not make a career or occupational *choice*. Instead of a career choice, implying a particular point in time, most sophisticated observers have recognized that there are a series of career-related decisions over a lifetime resulting in a person having a developmental career *pattern*. The process of developing a career is most complex. For example, it partly involves the reality testing of a person's self-concept. In effect, a person attempts to implement his self-concept through his life's work. For most however, the merger of one's self-concept with the realities of work often results in a compromise. In the following selection, an "old-new" teacher, one who has already invested 18 years in the business world, discusses the vagaries of his career development *pattern*.

Selection 9 TEACHING, WHERE HAVE YOU
BEEN ALL MY LIFE?

Teacher: Frank Karr
Age: 44
Experience: 19 months secondary; 18 years in several business activities

I'm a reasonably happy person today. But if someone were to have suggested to me 25 years ago that I would wind up as a teacher, I would have said, "Don't be absurd!" For me, its been a long, long time coming. And now that I'm teaching science here at Baldwin, my only regret is that I did not make the decision to enter teaching 20 years earlier. Oh, I know that it isn't so easy to get a job as a teacher these days, but I'm one of the lucky ones.

I'm *extremely* lucky. I'll be perfectly honest with you. What have I got to lose? The way I got this job is, that I got fired from my previous job in the business world. Fired! Yes, but through no fault of my own. See, there was a change in the management of the company. That's the way it is, my friend, out there in the cruel, tough world of business. One minute you're in, and the next minute you're out. Depends which way the wind is blowing and just where you happen to be standing at the time.

Anyhow, I've been teaching science here at Baldwin High School for the past year-and-a-half and I've loved every minute of it. The subject matter is right up my alley. I found that I can really hold the kids' attention. Teaching. It's really delightful. Frankly, it has never been like this for me before, on any job that I've held. I can hardly wait to get to work in the morning. And the faculty here is great. So helpful. So willing to share. My chairman, Mrs. Walters, will do most

131

anything to help out. Equipment, materials, supplies, and the most interesting ideas. What a wonderful working environment. As I said, I can hardly believe it. I have to pinch myself to make sure it's true. Excuse me.

Oh, I know that I'm a little too old to be so enthusiastic, but for me, finding myself has not been a simple matter. Some lucky people know immediately what they want to be. Somehow, they just know right off that they want to be a doctor, a lawyer, an artist, even a carpenter. So they go out and that's what they become. It's as simple as that.

But for me, it wasn't that natural. To be perfectly honest, I never dreamed I would be satisfied as a teacher. Ever since I can remember, from the time I was a little boy, I always dreamed of becoming a doctor. My parents wanted me to be a doctor, too. My father especially.

After high school, I went to the University of Pennsylvania as a premed student. Then the world began to close in on me. I was well into my junior year when it became obvious that I was not going to be able to get into medical school. My marks just weren't good enough. Mathematics was always very difficult for me and entrance into medical school in those days was extremely competitive. I just knew that I wouldn't be able to get in.

You can imagine what a blow that was. It wasn't just me. My mother and father were even more disappointed than I was. Well, naturally, I tried to salvage whatever I could. I finished my degree, with a biology major instead of premed. But as circumstances had it, there were no jobs available in biology per se.

I thought of teaching, and this was about 20 years ago don't forget, when almost any college graduate could step into a teaching job. Then, no sooner than I thought of it, I dismissed the idea as a bummer.

You see, I was about to get married, and the salaries they paid teachers in those days was a disgrace. So I took a job in business and enrolled in a graduate business program. I even studied law at nights for a year. But I wasn't able to find myself. I drifted from one business job to another. Claims, adjuster, life insurance sales. No go in any of them. Finally I settled on becoming a medical detailer, calling on doctors, mainly promoting new drugs. I never really liked it. In fact it was like rubbing salt in an old wound. Kowtowing to M.Ds. But I spent 12 hard years with the firm and made a fairly decent living, at least financially. Twelve years. Twelve years. As I look back on it, 12 years on a treadmill to oblivion. Fired, through no fault of my own. Management changed. You know the routine.

Then, as a last resort, I thought again of teaching. Oh, it wasn't easy going back to school and studying, with a lot of younger people, methods of teaching.

But I've been lucky. This job I have is by far the best work I've ever had in my life. It's helping people, it's using my mind, it's dignified. I love it. Teaching, where have you been all my life?

Suggestions for Further Study

1. Familiarize yourself with some of the theories regarding vocational development that are described in psychological and vocational guidance literature. Trace the career patterns of several experienced teachers and relate their experiences to the theories that you have reviewed.
2. What role do parents play in career development? Discuss.
3. Develop a panel composed of several different teachers and have them discuss "How and Why I Became a Teacher."
4. Interview a school administrator, a curriculum coordinator, and another *former* teacher and have them discuss "Why I left teaching."
5. Interview several of your classmates who intend to become teachers. Attempt to determine (a) their overt reasons for choosing teaching and (b) their covert (less obvious) reasons for choosing teaching as a profession.
6. What seemed to be the critical decisions in Frank Karr's life that lead to teaching as a career? Do you predict that he will remain as enthusiastic about his work 5 or 10 years later? Discuss.

Theme 10 Job Satisfaction

The rewards of teaching are for some, most elusive. Job satisfaction is often attributed to the extent that one's psychosocial needs are fulfilled from the job. All jobs inherently have the capacity to offer varying degrees of power, glory, prestige, and security as well as the satisfactions implicit in the character of the work itself. Concepts regarding job satisfaction—the joy of work and even the virtue of work—have been undergoing revision in a changing America. In the following vignette, Kurt Miller reflects on the rewards of teaching high school English, from his view. . . .

Selection 10   THE PAPER-MARKING AUTOMATON

Teacher: Kurt Miller
Age: 38
Experience: 15 years secondary (past 10 as school
   librarian)

It had become obvious to Kurt Miller that he was not finding adequate satisfaction in the teaching of high school English. In fact, he
concluded that his teaching had deteriorated into a tedious and
onerous chore.

He requested a transfer from his department chairman. "But
Kurt," his chairman said, "what's gone wrong? You seem so well-
equipped for the job. Is it the kids? Are they getting to you? Your
discipline seems very good. What is it?"

"Well," Kurt replied, "it's not the kids, in fact, I love them. And it's
not the subject matter because I love English, as you know. No, it's
neither of those. It's simply the endless stream of paperwork connected with the teaching of English that has taken my appetite away.
The paperwork is just incredible."

"Yes Kurt, I know," the chairman said compassionately, "but it's
so necessary."

"Certainly, but the constant drain from grading themes, every day,
week in and week out, is just too much. It's inhuman to expect,
especially if the teacher is more than halfway conscientious. I'm just
bloody sick and tired of marking papers four nights a week and all
day Sunday. Perhaps I wouldn't mind it as much if there were some
results from my efforts. But the kids don't seem to be learning to
write properly, in spite of all my efforts. The results just aren't there.
Where are the rewards of teaching? Where are the delicious fruits of

my efforts as a dedicated teacher? I'm sorry sir, but the rewards just aren't in the classroom, teaching English composition. Not at all."

"Is it really all that much?"

"Look. You should realize this more than anyone else. Five classes. One hundred-sixty children, each of whom, theoretically, writes a paper a week. Now each of these papers requires a considerable amount of time, comments, discussion, if they're to have any value at all to the students. In reality, I became an English teacher because, in a sense, I'm a literature buff. But do you know that for years now, ever since I took on this teaching job, I simply have not had the time or strength to read hardly any of the kind of literature that I enjoy. Oh no. Instead I read these inane, insipid, poorly written, carelessly done, high school themes. Do you realize what this is doing to my mind? And I know that it is dishonest, as well as useless for me to perpetuate the charade that I'm doing an effective job, either for my students or for myself. I've got to get out. I really do."

"I'm sorry to lose you Kurt, I really am. You are going to be a great loss."

"Well, sir. I've become nothing more than a paper-marking automaton. I think I have the potential to become more than that."

In due time, Kurt Miller did leave the classroom. He switched over to become the school librarian and began to again find the opportunity to read the kind of literature he enjoyed, no longer, as he put it, "a paper-marking automaton."

Suggestions for Further Study

1. Contrast the attitude toward teaching of Kurt Miller with that of Frank Karr in Selection 9. Consider the factors that cause one person to find satisfaction from his work, while another person finds a similar job quite distasteful. Review job satisfaction studies found in the literature of sociology, social psychology, and career education.

2. Develop a panel of several teachers, including at least one English teacher. Have the panel discuss their own job sat-

isfaction. If possible, ask the English teacher to reflect on the grading of themes.

3. What are some of the psychological needs that a person is able to satisfy through teaching? Which of your needs are not likely to be met through a teaching career, if any?

4. There is evidence to suggest that a person's values shift as he develops through various life stages. Will classroom teaching continue to mean the same thing to you and serve the same purposes for you in 10 or 15 years? Examine and discuss.

5. "Many teachers abandon the classroom." Examine (a) the validity of the preceding statement and (b) the causes, if true. What avenues are open for teachers who might wish to leave the classroom but remain in education?

Theme 11   The Professional Preparation of Teachers

What constitutes the optimal preparation of American teachers? Are the best teachers endowed at birth with the very qualities that make them so effective? Can the means to become truly effective in the classroom really be learned in college? How? Where? Certainly most teacher-education programs began with the premise that they had something useful to offer. Questions continue to arise, however. Is education an academic discipline worthy of advanced study? What changes in teacher education are eminent? What new directions *should* teacher education take? Max Forer, a young teacher, candidly reviews the quality of his own professional preparation.

Selection 11 TEACHER EDUCATION HAS A
LONG WAY TO GO

Teacher: Max Forer
Age: 23
Experience: 2 years elementary

The best course that I had in education wasn't really a course at all. It was the semester I spent student teaching. I was really on a tough job and had the full set of teaching responsibilities. The seminar we had at the college each week was directly related to problems that we were having on the job and it all made a lot of sense, even the theoretical stuff.

It's not that all my education courses up until student teaching made little sense. A few courses were quite interesting but only because the instructors were dynamic. But most of what they had to say had little application to the day-to-day realities of teaching, unfortunately. I say unfortunately because those of us in teaching really need all the help we can get. But we need relevant help, not theory.

I know many of the teachers that I'm working with here at Northside really resent many of the education courses that they took while in college. In the faculty room, I've heard some of them say that their education courses were from the bottom of the barrel.

Well, even for me, I must admit that the courses that I took as an education major were much easier than those in other departments. It's not just that they were easier. Most of them seemed to be rehashes of each other! After you've taken one good course in the foundations and another in some teaching methods and techniques, what else is left?

139

But more than that. Some of the college's professors who were preparing future teachers were the poorest example of teachers themselves. There was this teacher of my test-and-measurements course who gave a final exam that exemplified the worst practice in testing conceivable. The way the exam was written and administered, it couldn't be completed during the allotted time. Poor planning. Can you imagine what we students thought of him and his theories of testing.

And then, of course, there was the classic: the teacher who gave the lecture on "The Evils of the Lecture Method." Ironic? Not really. Typical is more like it.

And when one of these education teachers finally did find a decent method, they worked it to death. Like small-group work. It became the vogue. The blind leading the blind. And for that *we* paid the tuition. The college should have been paying us.

There was even one teacher who turned every course he taught into sensitivity-training sessions, whether the objectives of the course warranted it or not. He really was irresponsible. You'd think the dean or someone would have straightened him out.

That's another thing. Who teaches these college professors how to teach? Doesn't anyone supervise them? They need help as much as anyone.

I don't know. I really wonder if I learned anything at all worthwhile about teaching when in college. Well, I suppose education courses are necessary, especially if you want a teaching certificate from the state. But in my opinion, teacher education has a long way to go. . . .

Suggestions for Further Study

1. Trace the historical roots of teacher education in America. What are some of the similarities and differences in the *nature* of the professional preparation of lawyers, medical doctors, teachers, and other "professionals."
2. Max Forer stated, ". . . the courses that I took as an education major were much easier than those in other depart-

ments." Discuss. Can education become an academic discipline in the same sense that psychology, biology, or physical sciences are academic disciplines?

3. Is teaching a profession or a craft? Differentiate. Define "professional." Do all professions require study in institutions of higher education? What is your view regarding the use of paraprofessionals in teaching? How would their preparation differ from "professionals."

4. There is a serious consideration of "competency-based" certification for teachers rather than merely the successful completion of a certain number of courses. What are the essential competencies necessary for teaching, and how can these be accurately measured?

5. Review college catalogues and appropriate literature and attempt to ascertain the best teacher education programs in your state, the nation, the world. What criteria did you use in making your determination and why?

6. What special strengths would you hope to find in the faculty of the best teacher education programs?

7. What criteria would you suggest be used in the selection of education students? To what extent is intelligence important? Previous academic success? Previous achievement? Cite research evidence, where possible, that supports your view.

8. Arrange for some experienced teachers to discuss the quality of their professional preparation. Compare their views with the picture presented by Max Forer. Interview a medical doctor and/or lawyer and ask them to discuss the quality of their professional preparation. Compare both teachers and other professionals views toward the quality of their preparation.

Theme 12 Teacher-to-Teacher Relations

Schools are a social system replete with a complex network of interpersonal relationships, rites of passage, social hierarchies, and physical trappings. The teacher's relationship with his colleagues is often of major consequence—for both the teacher's personal *and* professional well-being. Collegial relationships within the department, in team teaching, in the faculty room, and sharing onerous study hall or lunch room duty are part and parcel of the teacher's professional existence. The school is also a political system, subject to the customary shifts in *power* common to most political structures. These shifts in power often create havoc with the established order. Such is the case in "Blake's Last Rite."

Selection 12   BLAKE'S LAST RITE

Teacher: Vincent Headly
Age: 40
Experience: 15 years, elementary and secondary

"I suppose that by now you have some idea of why I've called the four of you together this morning," said Sorenson, the new principal, leaning back slowly in his big executive chair.

"Yes, sir. We have a pretty good idea of what you are about to say, but we'd appreciate getting the picture in a straightforward fashion, right from you." That was Bruce Olson, senior member of the English department. The three other department members—Jane Fargo, Vince Headly, and Joe Cooper—acknowledged silently that Olson was to be their spokesman. It was already abundantly clear that Olson would be the natural successor to the department chairmanship once Henry Blake was "disposed of." The foursome already knew that old Blake had been asked by Principal Sorenson to step aside, to make way for the younger man. This meeting, then, with the English department minus Blake, was in all respects a ritual, a rite of passage, a cant.

Sorenson chanted, "Oh, old Blake was a good man, a devoted teacher, a scholar, mind you, a scholar." But it was time for a change. "New leadership, new policies, innovations in English, progress, the need for Blake's extrication. Yes, old Blake must go—but with honor!"

Vincent Headly pondered the ritual. Here we hold ceremony over the still-warm body of old Blake. Why doesn't one of us put a stop to this? How can we watch Blake go down this way. He's befriended us all in numerous ways over the years. Is this what we've come to?

143

We, the sacred seekers of truth. We, the educational humanists. By our absence of protest, we dishonor Blake's trust in us. This is our last chance to do honor; speak up, he urged himself.

He knew that abrasive conflict with Sorenson, the new principal, would severly jeopardize the job tenure he had been promised. Surely, one of the others, someone fully tenured would speak up, he hoped. Headly searched the faces of his colleagues. They were all smiling benignly at Sorenson, the present key to their professional futures. Olson, tight lipped, high aspiring, was nodding affirmatively at Sorenson's every gesture. Jane Fargo seemed to be feigning concern, while Cooper, who was often out of immediate contact, betrayed the very fact with his frozen stare.

Not much to rely on here, Headly lamented. He held no illusion of the school being a true democracy. The faculty's role was advisory, not binding. Yet if one of them could take issue with Sorenson's removal of Blake, it might, it just might make a difference.

Don't despair, Headly thought. Between men, it has always been, "What's in it for me?" Altruism? Altruism is only for the naive, the uninitiated. Teachers are no different than any other breed of man. Self-serving bastards all. But you would think it would be different for teachers somehow.

As Sorenson's chant droned on, "Blake's best interest is to step aside. . ." Headly thought back to the time when he, as a neophyte instructor at Berkeley, was comfortably seated in the faculty room. It was customary for the newest teachers to answer the door if someone knocked. He was told later never to sit in Mr. Marshak's chair again. Servitude. Foolish traditions.

His mind engaged itself on another time, another place. A school where the faculty shared openly with each other, where a spirit of cooperation and mutual goodwill prevailed. Ideas, materials, and curriculum guides were passed about freely. People treated each other as fellow humans, sharing openly with each other.

Suddenly, a thought occurred to Headly. Perhaps he should speak up and take a risk on old Blake's behalf. Maybe he could begin to turn Berkeley around.

"Mr. Sorenson, sir," he found his quivering voice saying, "I'd like to take exception with your plans for Mr. Blake." Sorenson, stopped chanting and looked with surprise toward Mr. Headly. . . .

Suggestions for Further Study

1. Vincent Headly was clearly disappointed in his colleagues. What social factors can contribute to such apparent indifference? What information can you find in the literature of sociology, cultural anthropology, or social psychology that can shed light on the social conditions portrayed in this case?

2. What other discordant interpersonal situations among teachers are encountered in the schools? What can be done to help alleviate such situations. Cite a specific situation and discuss. Compare the interprofessional climate, teacher-to-teacher, with doctor-to-doctor relationships in a hospital, or worker-to-worker relations in another industry. Is the school a unique social system? If so, in what ways? Discuss.

3. Role play Bruce Olson and Vince Headly discussing the scene that was portrayed in the case, approximately one hour after leaving Sorenson's office. Limit role playing to four minutes. Have each role player discuss his feelings immediately after the role playing has been terminated. Then have your class discuss the role played situation as it emerged.

4. With which person in the case did you most readily identify? Why?

Theme 13   The School Administration and the Teacher

It is not unusual for employees to harbor some resentments toward "the boss." Teachers, as one might expect, are no different in this regard. What is somewhat different for teachers, however, is the fact that they have great difficulty *accepting* being imbedded in the lower end of the pecking order in most educational hierarchies, as army privates in relationship to their superiors. More and more teachers consider this pattern to be inappropriate and offensive, pointing out they have high-level academic credentials plus relevant "front line" experience and therefore are sometimes more qualified to lead than their administrators. Some offended teachers have commented, "In schools, the further one moves from the actual classroom—a coordinator, a counselor, a principal, a superintendent—the more power, prestige, and financial support he seems to be awarded. The public apparently believes the educational hierarchy should be the same as found in the military, business or government. But it just isn't right."

Selection 13 DON'T ROCK FRANK COREY'S BOAT

Teacher: Ann Crawford
Age: 22
Experience: 17 months, secondary

"Hi, gorgeous. Just finishing up? Such dedication you new teachers have," Bob Hester addressed Ann Crawford as she struggled across the faculty parking lot, her arms overloaded with posters and art supplies. "Let me help you," he said, relieving her of some of her packages.

"Thanks, Bob. But what do you mean 'such dedication?' Aren't all teachers dedicated?" she asked wryly. "Actually, I don't have a choice, do I?"

"Not really, I suppose."

"Bob, this student art show has become a second full-time job. As if teaching five periods of art a day isn't enough."

"It's unfair, I know," Hester said. "But apparently that's the lot of the younger teachers here. My first couple of years here I took the minutes for the PTA Executive Board. Somehow I always forgot to show up at the regular PTA meetings to read them. 'Mr. Hester will now read the minutes.' Long embarrassed pause. 'Mr. Hester! Mr. Hester!' No Mr. Hester. I forgot to show up too many times, and I almost lost my teaching job here to boot."

"How Freudian, Bob!" Ann remarked. "Freud said that we only forget what we want to forget."

"True!"

"But for me it's different. I wouldn't mind running this art show if the damn administration would keep from interfering. It's Old Baggy Pants and his neurotic fears that make this job so difficult. Now he

147

wants us to change the theme. He thinks the theme is too controversial for high school, just because we're displaying a few abstract nudes and sex scenes. Hell, the kids are way beyond what we're displaying. 'But it's too controversial,' he said. So afraid. So spineless. Tell me, Bob, is this the kind of leadership we have in education? Is this the kind of man that gets to be principal?"

"Don't be too harsh on Frank Corey, Ann. I've known him a long time. I'll admit, he never was known for his spunk. But he has been a very hard worker. Ann, bear in mind that being the principal of this school is a terribly difficult job. He's got pressures on him from every direction."

"I know, I know. But it's difficult for me to sympathize with him. After all, he's *our* leader. He's supposed to be on the cutting edge of education. *Some* model!"

"But, remember young lady, most of the guys who have worked themselves up in school administration have sacrificed quite a bit. Don't forget that they were all classroom teachers themselves at one time and they gave that up."

"I know that. And that's just my point. If they *really* cared about teachers and teaching, they'd still be teaching, wouldn't they? The teachers' job is the most important one in education, not the job of the administrator. The principal may have to concern himself with discipline in the school, but from my view, that's where his responsibility ends. Old Baggy Pants is always claiming his hands are tied. He's always passing the buck."

"Look, Ann. Perhaps some of what you're saying is true. But try to understand Frank Corey. Frank Corey is basically a nice, gentle guy trying to stay ahead on a tough job. Try going along with him. He doesn't need to rock the boat, and neither do you.

"There's enough aggravation in the schools without trying to create more. Look at it this way. Frank Corey's got a tough enough job. Let's not complicate it with unnecessary controversy. Corey has paid heavy dues to get where he is today. He took all those necessary administration credits. He served his time in the classroom. He's spent seven years as an assistant principal here, and believe me, that's enough of a price in and of itself to pay. Corey went to the right meetings, said all the things that people wanted to hear, and now he's principal. Come on now. Let's not rock Frank Corey's boat, if we don't have to."

Suggestions for Further Study

1. To what extent does Ann Crawford seem to represent your attitude and prevailing teacher attitudes toward school administration in a school with which you are familiar? Discuss.
2. Interview several teachers regarding their "private attitudes" toward their principal. Compare their views. Examine the roots of their attitudes.
3. What qualities and competencies are essential in an effective school administrator? Which of these are most important in earning faculty respect? Support your views.
4. Are the public-relations roles of both teachers and school administrators mutually reinforcing? In what ways?
5. Set up the following role-playing situation in your class and discuss.
   Scene: The principal's office
   Role players: "Old Baggy Pants," the principal
                   Ann Crawford
                   Jack Owens, student
   Situation: The principal has called teacher and student to his office, attempting to persuade them to "make the show less controversial."

Theme 14   Teachers and Their Professional Affiliations

Most experienced teachers have identified with at least one of the two major professional educational organizations: the American Federation of Teachers or the National Education Association, the latter composing the largest group of professional public employees in the nation. In addition, administrators, curriculum specialists, paraprofessionals, school counselors, and subject area and grade-level specialists, for example, have in many instances formed their own, special organizations as well. Furthermore, teachers have devised informal organizations to serve varied social and professional interests. Teachers new and old are therefore faced with the dilemma of which, if any, formal and informal groups they should join. The various structures, philosophies, methods of operation, degrees of militancy, and goals of these groups should be carefully evaluated before choosing. Tina Foch shares her own position regarding the local association.

Selection 14   JUST A MATTER OF TIME

Teacher: Tina Foch
Age: 31
Experience: 10 years, elementary

There is no question at all about it, teachers have long been too powerless. But, I think the pursuit of power might be being carried a little bit too far these days. However, on the other hand, I must admit that having the AFT in this school district has brought new life into our teachers association. I'm seriously considering changing over to the union, but I'm not sure just what the right thing to do is. The question, as I see, it, has to do with being professional.

We've certainly made great strides these past years as teachers. When I first came into teaching, our salaries weren't half what they are today. And these salaries didn't go up by osmosis. They went up because teachers were willing to stand together and *demand* a fair and equitable wage. Years ago, we teachers had extra assignments: clubs, chaperone dances, all *without* extra pay. No other workers would have put up with that. All that's gone now, thanks, I contend, to a strong teachers association.

Today, as you know, entering the teaching profession is very competitive. Many more people want to be teachers than there are jobs. One of the reasons is that teaching has come to be considered a respectable, decent-paying profession. Oh, it wasn't considered dignified years ago to strike. But the profession's come a long way since then.

You see, in the days before we had strong collective bargaining, school administrators had a fantastic amount of arbitrary power over the everyday working lives of teachers. The school board here had control over how we should dress, where we should live, and even *how* we should behave after school hours. Teachers smoking, drinking, or doing anything fundamentally human was frowned upon.

But today, you can see for yourself, teachers are no longer as timid or fearful. We have a sound contract. We have a *strong* teachers' organization. No longer can we be arbitrarily assigned to washroom patrol or dismissed without cause. What used to be collective begging has become collective bargaining.

And there are other changes too. The public no longer pities the poor teacher. To the contrary, in many respects today, the teacher is envied. Oh, she may not be loved quite as much as she used to be, but at least she is respected.

Today all kinds of groups are organizing themselves. The parents have been well organized for years. So have the boards. For teachers, it has taken a long, long time. Actually, the difference between the association and the union are quite minimal. In fact, I don't think it really matters that much whether one joins the union *or* association. It's only a matter of time before they both merge anyway. . . .

Suggestions for Further Study

1. To what extent should teacher power be increased, in your view? What support can you find for your position? Check your statement with reference to the following:
   (a) effects on worker values
   (b) effects on students
   (c) economic factors
   (d) political and social factors
2. What is the history of the AFT? The NEA? What do you presume the future holds for these groups? Why?
3. Interview the chairman of the salary-negotiation committee of a local teachers' association and familiarize yourself with his view. Also, interview a member of a local board of edu-

cation with regard to his concerns about the local teachers' association. Compare views. Discuss.

4. To which formal and informal professional groups do teachers that you know belong? Ask them why. Which groups, if any, do you plan to join in the future? Why?

Theme 15 Tenure

Tenure for teachers is the source of continued controversy and subject to a great deal of misunderstanding. Tenure was originally conceived as a means to protect the teachers from infringement upon their academic freedom, rather than a lifetime guarantee of a job, as some argue it is.

For some critics of American schooling, tenure has been represented as symbolic of "the overinsulation of the education establishment, insulation against needed change." Tenure, according to some educators, was offered in place of reasonable salaries. Today, that position seems less tenable. For many teachers, erosion of their tenure privileges is a volatile issue. Yet, more and more, old tenure laws are being changed. Gloria Ritt, a principal, highlights the issue as she reviews her case against a teacher *without tenure.* . . .

Selection 15   HE DIDN'T BELONG HERE

Teacher: Gloria Ritt
Age: 47
Experience: 15 years, elementary and secondary
principal

Interviewer: How do you, as a principal, decide who should and who should not be permitted to continue to teach in your school, that is, to receive tenure?

Ms. R: Well, there are many different factors that are involved. You get a picture of a teacher from many different sources. Where not too many years ago we thought that a checklist of teacher qualities was the answer, and a formal written report after an observation, today we find that it is at many different levels that we evaluate a teacher. We still do visit teachers. We still have the formal observation, but we recognize that the observation is limited because you don't always get a true picture. You don't see a characteristic situation. Very often the children are acting differently, the teacher is acting differently. It's not a typical thing. But you get a feeling about a teacher through youngsters, through their response to a teacher. You get a feeling about a teacher from how other teachers regard him, how well they can work with him, whether they can give and take with him. You get a picture from parents, certainly. When parents request that their youngster going into a certain grade have a particular teacher, this means a lot. And you also get a picture from your everyday dealings with the teacher, the kind of conversation he has with you, the ideas that he brings to his department, the general attitude that he has about educational matters. We're get-

155

ting away from the idea that the only way you can evaluate a teacher is in terms of classroom performance. His whole outlook on life is important. How does he feel about kids? Does he treat them like human beings?

Interviewer: All right. Now you have, on your staff, all types of teachers. Some presumably are outstanding, others average and perhaps some below average or poor. How do you decide who fits these categories, and how can you substantiate or justify your decision?

Ms. R: The only way that you can prove anything is from what you observe yourself. And again, you have to take the sum total of many different things. Your observation, the feeling you get about the person, in and out of the classroom.

Interviewer: I see. Well, if you were going to dismiss a nontenure teacher, what shortcoming would the teacher most likely have?

Ms. R: First of all, the teacher must be *interested* in teaching. He must want to teach and he must show his desire to teach by getting to the job and doing the basic things first, which are to get to class on time, keep the class reasonably controlled, and do a competent job, that's the least, the very least. That's the minimum and then, he must rise from that point. Here's where initiative, enthusiasm, creativity, and motivation comes to play. If you don't have that minimum of the teacher wanting to come and wanting to do a decent job, he should not teach. He also has got to be able to relate to kids. He's got to talk to young kids today, not as of 1960, but as of today. And, I don't think it's that difficult. There are many, many, fine teachers who can talk to kids today.

Interviewer: Hmmm. But can you talk about a teacher that didn't make it here?

Ms. R: Yes, well, I can think of a teacher who in some respects, I think some supervisors would say he did a good job. He met the minimum requirements that I mentioned. He did get to class on time. He did run his class efficiently. He got his grades in. He certainly did all of the things you're supposed to do as an *efficient* teacher. But his problem was that he hated the kids. He was a misanthrope. He didn't like people. He was a loner. And this came through in the classroom. The student was invariably wrong before he was right. He had invariably done something to offend the teacher's pride. And as far as I could see, there was little reason for this person to stay in this school. He was getting nowhere with the kids. There was no positive feeling from the youngsters toward him. They didn't want to learn because of him. If anything, they wanted to escape from him.

Interviewer: From what aspects of the man did they want to escape?

Ms. R: From his negativism, his harsh personality, a constant desire to fight. He made everything into a personal confrontation, and the kids just weren't up to it. I had to say to him that I really felt that he didn't belong here. And, interestingly enough, he agreed with me.

Interviewer: That must be one of the more difficult parts of being an administrator. How did you go about firing this teacher?

Ms. R: Well, as soon as I realized that there were some things I didn't like, I started talking to him about them.

Interviewer: Excuse me, how long had he been here?

Ms. R: He had been here for three years. (Pause) And I indicated to him what I felt was the problem. I gave him some suggestions as to what he could do to remedy the situation. I gave him some examples, made provision for him to visit some other classes, and gave him a chance to evaluate himself and what he was doing. Surprisingly, when we had the conference in which I had to indicate that I would not be able to recommend him for rehiring, he came up with the conclusion, "Well, gee, I really don't belong here." An interesting postscript to all this; he has since become an administrator in another school district. So I don't know if this is typically what happens to teachers who don't make it in the classroom. . . .

Suggestions for Further Study

1. From the information available, do you agree with Ms. Ritt's decision to dismiss the teacher? What criteria were used? Were any of the criteria obscure or political in nature? What do you recommend toward improving the process of evaluating teachers for tenure? Cite references or theoretical positions that lend support to your recommendations.

2. Interview several supervisors of instruction regarding their method of evaluating teachers. Have them identify the significant criteria they use in arriving at decisions regarding the awarding of tenure.
3. Describe the nature of the school's political and social system and how it may shape the teachers' professional future.
4. Role play a conversation between Mr. Z., the teacher evaluated in this case and the principal. Set the scene in the principal's office. Mr. Z. asks the principal, "Why are you firing me?" Keep the role playing under four minutes, then discuss *feelings* of both parties and implications of what was said.

Annotated Bibliography

Ashton-Warner, Sylvia. *Teacher.* New York: Simon and Schuster, 1963. An autobiography of the author's experiences as a teacher of Maoris and children of English background in New Zealand. Through her teaching diaries she discusses her scheme of Organic Teaching. Although her work was primarily done with the very young child, her ideas can be applied to all children.

Harnack, Robert S. *The Teacher: Decision Maker and Curriculum Planner.* Scranton, Pennsylvania: International Textbook Company, 1968. A compact study of the teacher in the process of curriculum planning with special emphasis on the needs, responsibilities, and supportive services necessary for such development.

Kushel, Gerald. *Discord in Teacher-Counselor Relations.* Englewood Cliffs, New Jersey: Prentice Hall, 1967. Presents a series of vivid case studies that portray classroom teachers' attitudes toward guidance counselors in the public schools.

National Education Association. *Research Reports.* Washington, D.C.: The Association, 1969–1972. The various research reports of the NEA provide comprehensive data on a nationwide basis on some of the major problems confronting teachers, such as salary, tenure, and retirement.

Stinnett, T. M. *Professional Problems of Teachers.* London: The Macmillan Company, Collier-Macmillan, Limited, 1968. This text provides a good overview of the professional problems of teachers and is intended to provide information for college students preparing for teaching.

United States Department of Health, Education and Welfare. *Teacher Militancy, Negotiations and Strikes.* PREP Report No. 8, Washington, D.C.: United States Government Printing Office, 1972. Presents, in abstract form, some of the studies undertaken in the area of teacher militancy and trends in strike activity. The bibliographies are useful for further reference in the area.

A Review and a Look Ahead
Suggestions for Further Study

1. Which selections were of greatest interest to you? Why? What issues or special areas of education seem to be of particular significance to you? Discuss. What additional research do you expect to undertake to further illuminate your knowledge regarding areas identified above?
2. What issues or areas of significance do you think were slighted in this text? Interview several teachers regarding these slighted areas. Discuss.
3. What promise does teaching hold for *you* in the years ahead?

Best wishes for a successful career in teaching!

References

Section I   Background and Foundations of Teaching

Commager, Henry Steele. *The Nature and Study of History.* Columbus, Ohio: Charles E. Merrill, Inc., 1960.

Honigmann, John J. *The World of Man.* New York: Harper and Row, 1959.

Kneller, George F. (ed.) *Foundations of Education* (3rd ed.). New York: Wiley, 1971.

Martin, Richard and Reuben G. Miller. *The Nature and Study of Economics.* Columbus, Ohio: Charles E. Merrill, Inc., 1965.

Phenix, Phillip H. (ed.). *Philosophies of Education.* New York: Wiley, 1962.

Rose, Caroline B. *The Nature and Study of Sociology.* Columbus, Ohio: Charles E. Merrill, Inc., 1965.

Sorauf, Francis J. *The Nature and Study of Political Science.* Columbus, Ohio: Charles E. Merrill, Inc., 1965.

Section II   Today's Student

Angelino, H., J. Dollins and E. V. Mech. "Trends in the 'Fears and Worries' of School Children as Related to Socioeconomic Status and Age," *Journal of Genetic Psychology.* Vol. 89 (1956), 263–277.

Ausubel, D. P., H. M. Schiff and E. B. Gasser. "A Preliminary Study of Developmental Trends in Sociopathy: Accuracy of

Perception of Own and Others' Sociometric Status," *Child Development.* Vol. 23 (1952), 111–128.

Bereiter, C. and S. Engelmann. *Teaching Disadvantaged Children in the Preschool.* Englewood Cliffs, New Jersey: Prentice-Hall, Inc., 1966.

Broderick, C. B. and S. E. Fowler. "New Patterns of Relationships Between Sexes Among Adolescents," *Marriage and Family Living.* Vol. 23 (1961), 27–30.

————, and G. P. Rowe. "A Scale of Preadolescent Heterosexual Development," *Journal of Marriage and the Family.* Vol. 30 (1968), 97–101.

Crandall, V. G. and U. Bellugi. "Some Relationships of Interpersonal and Intrapersonal Conceptualizations to Personal Social Adjustment," *Journal of Personality.* Vol. 23 (1954), 225–232.

Deutsch, M. "The Disadvantaged Child and the Learning Process: Some Social, Psychological and Developmental Considerations," N.Y.: Columbia University, paper prepared for The Ford Foundation *Work Conference on Curriculum and Teaching in Depressed Urban Areas,* 1962.

Durkheim, Emile. *Suicide: A Study in Sociology.* Trans. by George Simpson (London, 1951).

Erikson, E. H. "The Problem of Ego Identity," *Journal of American Psychoanalytic Association.* Vol. 4 (1956), 56–121.

"Facts About Sexual Freedom," *Education Digest.* Vol. 34 (1968), 12–15.

Gesell, A., H. Thompson, and others. *The First Five Years of Life, Age Guide to the Study of the Preschool Child.* New York: Harper, 1940.

————, F. L. Ilg, and others. *The Child from Five to Ten.* New York: Harper, 1946.

————, F. L. Ilg, and L. B. Ames. *Youth: The Years from Ten to Sixteen.* New York: Harper, 1956.

Havighurst, R. A. *Developmental Tasks and Education.* N.Y.: Longmans, Green and Co., 1952.

Hertz, Sylvia. "Research Study on Behavior Patterns in Sex

and Drug Use on the College Campus," *Adolescence*. Vol. 5 (1970), 1–16.

Inhelder, B. and J. Piaget. *The Growth of Logical Thinking from Children to Adolescence*. N.Y.: Basic Books, 1958.

Jones, H. E. *Motor Performances and Growth*. Berkeley, Calif.: University of California Press, 1949.

————. "Adolescence in Our Society," *The Family in a Democratic Society*. Anniversary papers of the Community Service Society of New York. N.Y.: Columbia University Press, 1949.

Kvaraceus, W. C. *The Relationship of Education to Self Concept in Negro Children and Youth*. Medford, Mass.: Tufts University Press, 1963.

Long, B. H. and E. H. Henderson. "Self-Social Concepts of Disadvantaged School Beginners," American Psychological Association, 1966. Paper read at annual meeting.

McCandless, Boyd R. *Children Behavior and Development*. N.Y.: Holt, Rinehart and Winston, 1967.

Maslow, A. H. *Motivation and Personality*. N.Y.: Harper, 1954.

————. "A Theory of Human Motivation," *Psychological Review*. Vol. 50 (1943), 370–396.

Offer, D., D. Marcus and J. L. Offer. "A Longitudinal Study of Normal Adolescent Boys," *American Journal of Psychiatry*. Vol. 126 (1970), 917–924.

Parsons, Talcott. *The Social System*. (London, 1951), 301–306.

Reese, H. W. "Relationships Between Self Acceptance and Sociometric Choices," *Journal of Abnormal Psychology*. Vol. 62 (1961), 472–474.

Rosenthal, R. and L. Jacobson. *Pygmalion in the Classroom*. New York: Holt, Rinehart and Winston, Inc., 1968.

Russell, D. H. "What Does Research Say About Self-Evaluation," *Journal of Educational Research*. Vol. 46 (1953), 561–573.

Schonfeld, W. A. "Inadequate Masculine Physique as a Factor in Personality Development of Adolescent Boys," *Psychosomatic Medicine*. Vol. 12 (1950), 49–54.

Sears, P. S. and V. S. Sherman. *In Pursuit of Self Esteem: Case Studies of Eight Elementary School Children.* Belmont, Calif.: Wadsworth Publishing Co., 1964.

Seeman, M. "On the Meaning of Alienation," *American Sociological Review.* Vol. 24 (1959), 70.

Sorensen, R.C. *Adolescent Sexuality in Contemporary America.* New York: World Publishing Company, 1973.

United States Department of Commerce, Bureau of Census, Washington, D.C., 1969.

United States Dept. of Justice, Bureau of Narcotics and Dangerous Drugs, Hearings of the Subcommittee on Appropriations for 1971, Part I, *The Judiciary and Department of Justice,* p. 946, House of Representatives, 91st Congress, Second Session.

United States Dept. of Labor, Bureau of Labor Statistics, Washington, D.C., 1969.

Weikart, D. P. *Preschool Intervention: A Preliminary Report on the Perry Preschool Project.* Ann Arbor, Michigan: Campus Publishers, 1967.

Wein, Bibi. *The Runaway Generation.* New York: McKay, 1970.

Section III   The Process

Ausubel, D. P. *The Psychology of Meaningful Verbal Learning: An Introduction to School Learning.* New York: Grune & Stratton, 1963.

Biddle, B. J. "The Integration of Teacher Effectiveness Research," B. J. Biddle and W. J. Ellena (eds.), *Contemporary Research on Teacher Effectiveness.* New York: Holt, Rinehart and Winston, Inc., 1964, 1–40.

Bigge, Morris L. *Learning Theories for Teachers.* New York: Harper & Row, 1971.

Bloom, B. S. *Taxonomy of Educational Objectives, Handbook I.* New York: David McKay Co., Inc., 1956.

Brown, George Isaac. *Human Teaching for Human Learning: An Introduction to Confluent Education.* New York: The Viking Press, 1971.

Bruner, J. S. *Toward a Theory of Instruction.* Cambridge, Mass.: Harvard University Press, 1966.

Buber, Martin. *The Knowledge of Man.* N.Y.: Harper & Row, 1965.

Bugelski, Bergen R. *The Psychology of Learning Applied to Teaching* (2nd ed.). N.Y.: Bobbs-Merrill Co., 1965.

Clayton, Thomas E. *Teaching and Learning: A Psychological Perspective.* Englewood Cliffs, New Jersey: Prentice-Hall, 1965.

Cogan, M. L. "The Behavior of Teachers and the Productive Behavior of Their Pupils: I. 'Perception' Analysis, II. 'Trait' Analysis," *Journal of Experimental Education.* Vol. 27, (1958).

Combs, A. W. and D. Snygg. *Individual Behavior, A Perceptual Approach to Behavior* (rev. ed.). N.Y.: Harper & Row, 1959.

Costin, Frank, W. T. Greenough, and R. J. Menges. "Student Ratings of College Teaching: Reliability, Validity and Usefulness," *Review of Educational Research.* Vol. 41, (1971), 511–535.

Dewey, John. "The Reflex Arc Concept in Psychology," *Psychological Review*, III, 1896, 357–370.

Emlaw, R., R. Mosher, N. Sprinthall, and J. Whitely. "Teacher Effectiveness: A Method for Prediction and Evaluation," *National Elementary Principal.* Vol. 43 (1963), 38–49.

Flanders, N. A. "'Teacher Influence, Pupil Attitudes and Achievement," Minneapolis: University of Minnesota, College of Education, November 30, 1960. (Final Report, Cooperative Research Project #397, U.S. Office of Education.)

———. "Some Relationships Among Teacher Influence, Pupil Attitude and Achievement," B. J. Biddle and W. J. Ellena (eds.) *Contemporary Research on Teacher Effectiveness.* New York: Holt, Rinehart and Winston, Inc., 1964.

Gage, N. L. "Paradigms for Research on Teaching," *Handbook on Teaching.* Chicago: Rand McNally, 1963, 94–141.

———. "An Analytical Approach to Research on Instructional Methods," *Phi Delta Kappan,* Vol. 49 (1968), 602.

———. *Teacher Education and Teacher Effectiveness: The Search for a Scientific Basis.* Palo Alto: Pacific Books, 1970.

Gagne, Robert M. *Conditions of Learning.* N.Y.: Holt, Rinehart and Winston, 1970.

Highet, Gilbert. *The Art of Teaching.* N.Y.: Knopf, 1950.

Hilgard, Ernest R. *Theories of Learning.* N.Y.: Appleton-Century-Crofts, Inc., 1956.

———. "Theories of Learning and Instruction," *The 63rd Yearbook of the National Society for the Study of Education.* Chicago: University of Chicago Press, 1964.

Kuethe, James L. *The Teaching-Learning Process.* Glenview, Illinois: Scott, Foresman and Co., 1968.

Lewin, Kurt. *Resolving Social Conflicts.* N.Y.: Harper & Bros., 1948.

McGee, H. M. "Measurement and Authoritarianism and Its Relation to Teachers' Classroom Behavior," *Genetic Psychology Monographs.* Vol. 52 (1955), 89–146.

Mosher, Ralph. "Teacher Effectiveness: Implications for Research on Counselor Selection and Effectiveness," John M. Whitely (ed.), *Research in Counseling.* Columbus, Ohio: Charles E. Merrill Publishing Co., 1967.

Perls, Fritz. *Gestalt Therapy Verbatim.* Lafayette, Calif.: Real People Press, 1969.

Rogers, Carl R. *Freedom to Learn.* Columbus, Ohio: Charles E. Merrill Publishing Company, 1969.

Rockeach, M. "The Nature and Meaning of Dogmatisms," *Psychological Review.* Vol. 61 (1954), 194–204.

———. *The Open and Closed Mind.* New York: Basic Books, 1960.

Ryans, P. G. *Characteristics of Teachers.* Washington, D.C.: American Council on Education, 1960.

Simon, Sidney B., L. W. Howe, and H. Kirshenbaum. *Value Clarification*. New York: Hart Publishing Co., 1972.

Sprinthall, N., J. Whitely and R. Mosher. "Prediction and Evaluation of Teacher Effectiveness at the Secondary School Level," Cooperative Research Project, #S-143 U.S. Office of Education, Dept. of Health, Education and Welfare, Washington, D.C., 1964.

—————. "A Study of Teacher Effectiveness," *Journal of Teacher Education*. Vol. 28, No. 1 (1966), 93–106.

Thorndike, Edward L., and R. S. Woodworth. "The Influence of Improvement in One Mental Function Upon the Efficiency of Other Functions," *Psychological Review*. (May, 1901), 247–261; (July, 1901), 384–395; (November, 1901), 553–564.

—————, and Elizabeth Hagen. *Measurement and Evaluation in Psychology and Education*. New York: Wiley, 1969.

Yee, A. H. "Is the Minnesota Teacher Attitude Inventory Valid and Homogeneous?" *Journal of Educational Measurement* (1967), 151–161.

Section IV   The Teacher

National Education Association. *Changes in Teacher Education: An Appraisal*, National Commission on Teacher Education and Professional Standards, Report of the Columbus Conference, The Association, Washington, D.C. (1964).

—————. *Grievance Procedures for Teachers in Negotiations Agreements*, NEA Research Report, No. R-8, The Association, Washington, D.C. (1969), 5–13.

—————. *Teacher Supply and Demand in Public Schools 1970*, NEA Research Report, No. R-14, The Association, Washington, D.C. (1970), 5.

—————. *Research Bulletin*, Vol. 50, No. 1, The Association, Washington, D.C. (1972), 3–7, 30.

————. *Teacher Retirement Systems*, The Association, Washington, D.C. (1972), 6.

————. *Teacher Tenure and Contracts*, No. R-11, The Association, Washington, D.C. (1972), 7.

Woellner, Elizabeth H. *Requirements for Certification*. Chicago, 1972.

Appendix A
Guide to "Answer-Finding" in Education

Students of education seeking "answers" to questions about teaching or other aspects of education are recommended the following procedure:

At the outset, it is quite common that the student finds he is a bit hazy in knowing exactly what he is seeking. For this reason, it is necessary that he or she spend sufficient time and energy developing an "answerable" question. Your professor or some of your fellow students can often help you with this essential first step. Perhaps, at first, you simply can manifest a general interest in an issue or a concept. Assume, for example, that you're interested in the construct called "teaching." After some serious thinking and deliberate browsing in book indexes, bibliographies, and tables of contents of education texts, the interest in the term "teaching" may result in the question: "Just what is teaching, anyway?" This can very well be the beginning of serious, self-directed inquiry and research. Periodically, throughout the inquiry process, the question will require a redefinition and refinement. You will probably find that your original question was much broader than you had expected, and in order to execute your inquiry within a reasonable period of time, the boundaries of the question will need to be delimited and made much more specific. For example, the question regarding teaching might eventually emerge as follows: "Does the teaching of mathematics in Monroe Elementary School require that a teacher be present in the classroom most of the time?"

The researcher might begin his inquiry by consulting subject cards in the library card index. Background and review of previous research on the topic is often essential. Empirical type information from the *Encyclopedia of Educational Research* offers an invaluable assist with this aspect of the inquiry. This book's index can lead into a fertile source of research articles appropriate to the user's topic or question, however, it should be noted that this volume is updated only every 10 years or so. To supplement and update what is found here, the student should turn to *The Review of Educational Research*, which is now issued quarterly each year, focusing thoroughly on selected educational topics in each volume. Begin with the most recent issue devoted to the topic you have in mind. The many references listed at the end of pertinent articles cited in either of these research compilations often act as further sources.

If the focus is not necessarily limited to research-type data, the *Education Index* can sometimes prove helpful. This index affords a listing of research and opinion articles found in approximately 200 educational periodicals and many yearbooks, bulletins, and monographs published in the United States, Canada, and Great Britain. When using this index, it is usually most profitable to begin with the most recent volumes and search back to earlier editions when and if necessary.

Many other useful indexes are available. Some likely to be pertinent for students in education are *Psychological Abstracts*, which offers summaries of psychological reports with the December issue providing a cumulative annual author and subject index; *Child Development Abstracts and Bibliography*, issued every four months; *Dissertation Abstracts*, which alphabetically lists doctoral dissertations accepted by over 143 colleges and universities; and *Sociological Abstracts*, which abstracts articles and book reviews from several hundred periodicals, domestic and foreign, five times a year.

For a bibliography relating to a general topic, the student should consult the *Bibliographic Index*, issued semiannually. It is, in effect, a comprehensive bibliography.

Other general sources especially appropriate to education are *Educator's Encyclopedia, The International Encyclopedia of Social Sciences, The Annual Review of Psychology, Standard Education Almanac*, and the *Dictionary of Education*.

The World Year Book of Education is useful for questions dealing with international education. Handbooks such as *The Handbook of Research on Teaching,* which covers in scope nursery school to college, and the *Handbook of Educational Research on Teacher Effectiveness* also can readily provide the inquirer with appropriate information.

A most important recent aid to researchers is the development by the U.S. Office of Education of the Educational Research Information Center (ERIC). ERIC is a national information retrieval system consisting of a number of regional clearinghouses that collect, abstract, and index most available educational information. Students can contact ERIC offices in Washington, D.C. for an index of materials related to their area of inquiry. In addition, ERIC publishes a monthly journal, *Research in Education,* which indexes abstracts and describes documents in the ERIC collection. Copies are available in many libraries or by individual subscription with the U.S. Government Printing Office in Washington, D.C. Documents are available in hard copy pages or on microfiche and can be ordered from the ERIC Document Reproduction Service, 4936 Fairmont Avenue, Bethesda, Maryland, 20014.

The U.S. Government Printing Office continuously issues a wide variety of bulletins on educational statistics. Your college library also has government documents, especially those issued through the U.S. Office of Education, that can be quite relevant to your inquiry. In short, there is no limit to the means by which an energetic student can search for "answers" to questions resulting from consideration of folklore and fact from experienced teachers.

Bibliography for the Guide to "Answer-Finding"

Bereday, George A. and Joseph A. Lauwerys (eds.). *The World Yearbook Encyclopedia.* New York: Harcourt, Brace and Jovanovich, Inc. (1966).

Bibliographic Index. New York: H. W. Wilson (1937—).

Biddle, B. J. and W. J. Ellena (eds.). *Contemporary Research on Teacher Effectiveness.* New York: Holt, Rinehart and Winston, Inc. (1964).

Chall, L. P. (ed.). *Sociological Abstracts.* New York: Eastern Sociological Society and the Midwest Sociological Society (1952).

Child Development Abstracts and Bibliography. Washington, D.C.: National Research Council of the Society for Research in Child Development (1927—).

Dissertation Abstracts. Ann Arbor, Michigan: University Microfilms, Inc. (1938—).

Ebel, Robert (ed.). *Encyclopedia of Educational Research.* New York: Macmillan Company (1969).

Gage, N. L. (ed.). *The Handbook of Research on Teaching.* Chicago: Rand McNally (1963).

Good, Carter V. *Dictionary of Education.* New York: McGraw-Hill (1959).

Handbook of Educational Research. Tyrus Hillway, Boston: Houghton Mifflin (1969).

Loevinger, J. (ed). *The Annual Review of Psychology.* Stanford, California: Annual Reviews (1939).

Psychological Abstracts. Washington, D.C.: American Psychological Association (1931—).

172

Renetzky, Alvin and Jon S. Greene (eds.). *Standard Education Almanac*. Los Angeles: Academic Media, Inc. (1968—).

Research in Education, U.S. Government Printing Office, Washington, D.C. (1967—).

The Review of Educational Research. Washington, D.C.: American Educational Research Association (1931—).

Sills, David L. (ed.). *The International Encyclopedia of Social Sciences*. New York: Macmillan Company and the Free Press (1968).

Smith, Edward W., Stanley W. Krouse, and Mark M. Atkin. *The Educator's Encyclopedia*. Englewood Cliffs, New Jersey: Prentice-Hall (1961).

Towner, Isabel L. (ed.). *Education Index*. New York: Wilson (1929—).

INDEX

175